LIFE
—between—
Sundays

LIFE
—between—
Sundays

HOW TO OVERCOME
CHALLENGE AND ADVERSITY
EVERY DAY

JOSEPH W.
WALKER III

DESTINY IMAGE® PUBLISHERS, INC.

P.O. Box 310, Shippensburg, PA 17257-0310

"Speaking to the Purposes of God for This Generation and for the Generations to Come."

This book and all other Destiny Image, Revival Press, MercyPlace, Fresh Bread, Destiny Image Fiction, and Treasure House books are available at Christian bookstores and distributors worldwide.

For a U.S. bookstore nearest you, call 1-800-722-6774.

For more information on foreign distributors, call 717-532-3040.

Or reach us on the Internet: www.destinyimage.com

ISBN 10: 0-7684-2829-7
ISBN 13: 978-0-7684-2829-2

For Worldwide Distribution, Printed in the U.S.A.

2 3 4 5 6 7 8 9 10 11 / 13 12 11 10 09

Dedication

This book is dedicated to my "Puffin," Diane Greer-Walker. From your first breath until your body rested and your spirit soared, you brought joy and encouragement to so many. May your memory live on, and may multitudes be touched through this written record of our special union and all that I've learned before, during, and after our extraordinary 11-year pilgrimage together.

Although the true meaning of the nickname "Puffin" will forever remain our little secret, you really were like a puffin bird in so many ways. The puffin is distinct among birds in its ability to go on long foraging trips, bringing back an abundance of food (energy) for its offspring. The distant journeys you went on with God and His Word, always bringing back an immeasurable supply of goodness and boundless energy to share with us all, typified your life.

Even in the midst of your pain and struggle, you never stopped voyaging into the light for the true manna. If only I had known which excursion would be your last, I would have doubtless insisted on tagging along. Instead, I remain.

In remembrance of you, I've penned this modest tome in hopes of finding some beauty in the ashes of losing you. And to you, my Puffin, now free from the confines of this world, I say, *"Fly!"*

Acknowledgments

I am grateful to the entire Greer family, who gave me their blessing in sharing intimate details of Diane's life and legacy in order to encourage the world: Your blessings will never be forgotten.

To my parents: I am so grateful that I have a mother who moved to Nashville for several months to assist me during the most difficult time of my life. I am also blessed to have a straight-talk father who never let me lose sight of what was important in life.

To all of my siblings: You are a blessing, and I am eternally grateful for your love and support.

To the Mount Zion Baptist Church of Nashville, Tennessee: Your continued support and love over the years has been incredible. Leading a church with such a heart for God remains my biggest blessing.

To Andrea and Carl Willis: Thank you, Carl, for giving of your time and resources to be available to Diane during her illness. She loved you, and I do as well. Andrea, thank you for being a sister and friend to us both. You went over and beyond the call of duty. Your gift of friendship will always be appreciated.

To Karl Rogers: You will never know what your kindness meant to us. I am convinced that God made us neighbors during that season because you and your family were our angels. Thanks.

To David Smallwood: You will never know how appreciative I am for your dedication to this project. You helped me capture the story in ways I would have never been able to articulate.

To Michelle S. Duffie: Your passion for marketing this project and seeing it through from beginning to end made the difference. Your spirit of excellence is unmatched.

To Gilda's Club of Nashville, Tennessee: Thank you! The support groups got me through. It was a true blessing to be able to share in a group with some of the most courageous and giving people I have ever met. Keep doing what you do. It works!

To Pastor Harry Blake, my pastor: Your words of insight continue to usher me toward my destiny.

To Bishop Eddie L. Long, whose sacrifice and friendship will never be forgotten: You are truly a brother and a friend. Your word to me in the midst of my pain shifted me to a new calling to the world.

To Bishop Paul S. Morton and Pastor Deborah Morton: I love you both and thank God for your spiritual covering. You are amazing—a consistent reminder of what is possible through the storm.

Finally, to all of you who will read this book: Thank you for taking time to hear this story. I pray that my experience and candor moves you to a place of faith like never before. It is my prayer that, no matter what happens *between* your Sundays, your life is enriched every time Sunday comes.

Endorsements

To use well-known words, my friend Joe Walker has "touched the bottom and found it sound." And now he has written and described the experience.

You want to listen carefully to people like Joe Walker. They carry the credentials of suffering; they've heard God's voice in the darkness. So you learn from them, and you are changed because of what they say into your soul. Joe Walker's book *Life Between Sundays* will make all of that happen. You can't afford to miss a single page.

> DR. GORDON MACDONALD
> Interim President, Denver Seminary,
> Editor-at-Large, *Leadership Journal*
> Speaker, Teacher, Author of *Ordering Your Private World*

"Why?" That seems to be our first response to life's tragedies and traumatic experiences, which exempt no one. Joe Walker is not afraid to ask that question, but he does not stop there. Etchings of God's finger on the tablets of his heart have left indelible lessons to help us grow and mature. Learning those lessons for himself is one thing, sharing those with others is a nexus of pain and courage. Thanks for both.

> DR. SAMUEL R. CHAND
> www.samchand.com
> Leadership Consultant and Author

Life Between Sundays is an honest and powerful story about the journey of two of the Lord's humblest servants. Joseph and Diane channeled their pain into hope and their hardship into inspiration. Their story is one of actionable faith—something all of us should practice more of.

HAROLD FORD JR.
U.S. Senate Candidate
MSNBC Political Correspondent and
Former Tennessee Congressman

If your endurance has ever been tested, *Life Between Sundays* is a must-read for you. Bishop Walker shares the story of his wife's fight against cancer and crafts it into a psalm of hope and renewal. This book is a superbly written metaphor for the period between the good times. It proves to readers that when devastating things happen, God has a prognosis for you, a plan to bring you out and a purpose for it all.

BISHOP EDDIE L. LONG
Senior Pastor, New Birth Missionary Baptist Church,
Atlanta, GA

How Do I Love Thee?

How do I love thee? Let me count the ways.
I love thee to the depth and breadth and height
My soul can reach, when feeling out of sight
For the ends of Being and ideal Grace.
I love thee to the level of every day's
Most quiet need, by sun and candlelight.
I love thee freely, as men might strive for Right;
I love thee purely, as they turn from Praise.
I love thee with the passion put to use
In my old griefs, and with my childhood's faith.
I love thee with a love I seemed to lose
With my lost saints,—
I love thee with the breath,
Smiles, tears, of all my life!—and, if God choose,
I shall but love thee better after death.

—ELIZABETH BARRETT BROWNING,
"Sonnet 43" of Sonnets From the Portuguese

Table of Contents

SECTION I
Sunday—THE SPIRITUAL

SECTION II
Monday—THE SOULFUL

SECTION III
Tuesday—THE PHYSICAL

SECTION IV
Wednesday—THE EDUCATIONAL

SECTION V
Thursday—THE VOCATIONAL

SECTION VI
Friday—THE FINANCIAL

SECTION VII
Saturday—THE RELATIONAL

SECTION VIII
THE TRUTH IN THE DARK

Foreword

Dr. Joseph Walker, with an immensely practical yet deeply spiritual insight that crosses denominational, racial, gender, societal, and economic barriers, illustrates his own intimate experience with an unexpected setback, the death of his beautiful wife, Diane. With compassionate wisdom and refreshing honesty, Dr. Walker shares his journey in life, which includes coming to grips with death and all that it represents.

Somehow, this passionate writer—who is also a theologian, civic leader, and entrepreneur—has the gift of approaching a subject many run from: how to help others see that some blessings only come by way of affliction. Now some of you may wonder: What blessings can be found in such a devastating time and season of life? Your beloved spouse dies, and there are blessings? Your beloved spouse dies, and there is hope for a great future? Your beloved spouse dies, and you can even imagine the strength and courage to help others while so desperately needing help yourself? What does Dr. Walker have that so many others need? Is it strength? Is it courage? Is it some hidden truth available only to a handful? Or, does he have the ability to understand that often life's *mess* plus *age* (time) becomes a *message* that will benefit others walking where he once walked!

Now it's one thing to go through such tough experiences; but can you even imagine having to lead the troops when you are wounded yourself? This book is not for wimps! This book is not for weak, bratty complainers. This book is for those of us looking for a guidebook that goes beyond telling "a sad story" and instead uses the most painful, most awful, most troubling issues of life and death to provide renewed strength, comfort, hope, and courage!

BISHOP PAUL S. MORTON SR.
Senior Pastor, Changing a Generation, Atlanta, GA
Co-Pastor, Greater St. Stephen Ministries,
New Orleans, LA
Presiding Bishop, Full Gospel Baptist Church
Fellowship International

Introduction

Life's setbacks are never accidental. They are always a piece of a larger landscape—distinct, metaphorical scenes in an epic masterpiece. A metaphor is "a thing regarded as representative or symbolic of something else; something abstract." At first glance, a book entitled *Life Between Sundays* might lead your mind to evoke images of "a week in the life" of someone or something. Taken at face value, you'd be quite right. But metaphorically speaking, *Life Between Sundays* represents so much more than the sun's rising one Sunday morning and its customary journey over the horizon seven days later. As citizens of this great earth, it's usually "between Sundays" that we become most intimately acquainted with the realities of being human among humans, both the tender and the terrifying.

In many cultures, Sunday is often associated with a day of reprieve from what's going on in the rest of the world—a day when you can legitimately say, "Time-out, world! I'm off today. I'll see you on Monday!" And when looking at Sunday through a metaphorical lens, it can be any day of the week that represents a day of rest.

It's what happens between one day of rest and the next, one week later, that I refer to as the "life between Sundays." For those with religious convictions, Sunday is typically the day when you cease from most activities, except for honoring the Creator in some way (prayer, church, Bible study), and take some much needed time to unwind. Your Sunday ritual may include attending a church or worship service, perhaps partly to find comfort from the past week's battles, and more

19

likely, to find strength for the ones ahead. For the not-so-religious, Sunday is still closely associated with pausing from all work—a time to recuperate and recharge for the coming week. Across many of the world's social, religious, and cultural landscapes, Sunday is character-ized as a day of much-deserved rest and rejuvenation as a result of what's transpired between Sundays.

WHAT A "WEEK" REPRESENTS

Now that I've piqued your curiosity about metaphors, days of rest, and what happens between them, let's talk a little bit about why I'm writing this book and how it applies to your life and mine. Throughout this book, references to specific days of the week, or an entire "week," should not always be viewed literally. They should be understood as representations of specific periods of time in your life that vary in dura-tion depending on the situation to which you apply them.

We all know that some weeks are harder and seem to stretch on longer than others. I've had seven-day weeks that felt like seven months in a concentration camp. I've also had weeks that felt like they passed in seven hours. For some reason, and maybe you can relate, those seven-hour weeks usually come along when I'm vacationing in Miami Beach, or strolling along the Brazilian coastline. It is also plausible to say that when we talk about a "week," it doesn't always have to equate to seven literal days, but can refer to a more figurative season of time ranging from several days to several years. I'll share a short story to illus-trate my point:

Many years ago, a member of my church named Anthony was accused of a crime he did not commit. Despite Anthony's pleas of inno-cence, he appeared before a judge one Monday morning, and by lunchtime he was facing 25-to-life. His whole future was revised with one stroke of the gavel. But then, six months into Anthony's sentence, an anonymous tip led authorities to the real perpetrator, who confessed to the crime. The following Monday morning, exactly six months after his sentencing, Anthony went before the same judge. This time, the striking of the gavel amended Anthony's future and granted his freedom.

I was there when Anthony hurried under a canopy of razor wire, marching toward the exit that consummated his freedom. The very first thing he said was, "I was sentenced on a Monday and released on a Monday. Doc, that was the longest and hardest *week* of my life!" Anyone even vaguely familiar with Anthony's story knew precisely what *week* he was referring to—that distressing six months he spent behind bars, wrongfully accused.

This book is about a "week" like Anthony's, when one event threatens to uproot the landscape of your future. More precisely, it's about several "weeks" like Anthony's—weeks with definitive beginnings and endings, but also ones that encompass much more in length and breadth than seven calendar days.

The weeks in this book are *my* weeks, my experiences, yet I trust that you will also see your own life's journey reflected in these pages. I pray that you will find comfort, hope, and a fresh understanding of God as you read. Because above all else, though many titles have been associated with my name over the years (doctor, pastor, teacher, civic leader, entrepreneur), in these pages, I'm writing to you as Joe Walker, friend and encourager.

TURNING PERSONAL PAIN INTO ENCOURAGEMENT

On Sunday, January 16, 2005, my "week" changed—*forever*. And as a result, so did my life. If you've ever had a catastrophe rudely invade the normalcy of your existence, you know the exact kind of finality I mean when I say *forever*. It was on that particular Sunday that my beloved wife, Diane Greer-Walker, died after an 18-month battle with pancreatic cancer.

Hold on. Don't put the book down so fast. This isn't another doom and gloom cancer story that's bound to leave you depressed, hoping and praying you never get cancer. Don't get the disturbing feeling that somehow reading about it might make you more susceptible to it. It's taken me more than three years to pen this book because I made myself a promise that it wouldn't be that kind of book. It had to be a book about journeying through the tumult of the situation, but more importantly, living victoriously on the other side of it.

I'll be the first to admit that after Diane died, there were times when I would come home and turn on the light switch, but the room would still be dark. The illumination from the large chandelier over our dining room table had flooded the room, but darkness still smothered my soul. For nearly a year, I meticulously laid out table settings for two, and often had conversations with Diane, as I sat alone in the darkness of our brightly lit dining room.

It was those shadowy times that led me to seek counseling. It wasn't counseling for Bishop Joseph Warren Walker III, but simply counsel for Joe Walker, a man with a wounded heart who needed some help navigating through grief's black tunnel. But get through it I did, which is why I'm on the other side now, still feeling the dull ache of love lost, but healthy and healed enough to pen this modest tome.

Diane was such an amazing woman that when she died, the thing I wanted to do more than anything else was to tell her life story and honor my baby's legacy. But I wasn't sure exactly how to proceed. I didn't want it to be just another run-of-the-mill biography, a book detailing a wonderful woman's life that, in all reality, is only relevant and interesting to family members and a few friends.

What I struggled with for extended periods of time was how I could write about the life of my beloved wife, someone near and dear to my heart, in a way that's not only interesting, but also delivers encouragement and empowerment to a broad spectrum of people. Of course, to me, Diane was my queen, an awesome woman, someone I wanted the whole world to know about. I wanted to shout about her from the rooftops.

On the other hand, you know as well as I do that reading stories about the lives of others whom you know little or nothing about can be like reading the obituaries—the longer they are, the less likely you are to read them through till the end. You may scan the first couple of sentences to see when someone was born and when they died. Beyond that, little else is of interest to you, unless a sentence jumps out about *how* they died. Then you'll read that paragraph on your way to the wastebasket.

Isn't it funny how we only respond that way with people we consider ordinary or uninteresting? Anytime we find out that a celebrity or famous athlete died, we read every last detail of the obituary or editorial account of their lives. Afterward, we go out and buy *People* magazine and *US Weekly* and read about it again. Then we get on the Internet, when we should be working, and scan Web pages for more juicy tidbits. If a book is later released about that person's life, we run to the bookstore, gladly turn over $25, and devour all the "extra" facts we missed from the cursory coverage.

You can probably see where I'm going with this. To those closest to us, Diane was a wonderful woman and leader. And while she was known as the "First Lady" of our church—Mount Zion Baptist Church in Nashville, Tennessee—she wasn't Princess Diana. (Well, she was *my* Princess Diane.) But did that mean her story wasn't one worth telling? Absolutely not! For me, the question was how to tell her story and when, not if.

As I pondered my predicament, I began to think back to how the experience of Diane being diagnosed and battling cancer stripped me down to a place of humanity where I had to come to some heart-wrenching determinations about what was truly important in life. I had to examine every aspect of my being and determine what was worth fighting for, and what was a pointless distraction attempting to keep me from mere survival. During that time of painful introspection, four things surfaced as key insights:

1. Diane's illness forced me to do a traumatic, dissecting inventory of every facet of my life.

2. While doing that inventory, I discovered some very significant lessons and truths that I knew would be beneficial, not only to my own personal growth, but also to the lives of others.

3. My experiences before, during, and after Diane's illness all played a vital role in uncovering and shaping those lessons.

4. The stories (humorous, tragic, and intimate) that made those lessons so significant and critical to my survival could be utilized as wonderful illustrations and reinforcements for making them applicable to the lives of others.

And it was upon the discovery of those four key insights that I knew there was a book inside of me that just might be of interest to more than 12 people.

I had cleared the first hurdle of figuring out how to tell Diane's story in a relevant and meaningful way. The next step was to figure out how to break the one big lesson of dealing with the agony of Diane's illness and death into digestible slices of wisdom for the world. It appeared I needed to spend a few more months in the closet of introspection.

While it's never fun spending time alone in a dark closet, it's amazing what you find in there once you get beyond the fear of being alone in a dark closet. The light does come on eventually, and you discover what a wondrous place it is in God to be alone, but not alone, whether or not the light is on.

Before I get too deep, let me tell you what came of those lengthy times of pondering. I recognized that while the key insights and Thematic Touchpoints were the first step in having something of substance to share with others, I also discovered seven significant areas of my life. I refer to these as "Focal Points" because they became the focus of my introspection during the most difficult times.

> *A Thematic Touchpoint is a key life lesson that I learned in the midst of a difficult circumstance, a lesson that is general enough in theme for you to apply to your own tough situations. Look for these boxes throughout this book. The Thematic Touchpoints will help you immediately apply the key life lessons you are learning about to life's toughest questions.*

SEVEN FOCAL POINTS:

1. **The Spiritual**—my personal relationship with God

2. **The Soulful**—the state of my mind, will, and emotions

3. **The Physical**—an assessment of my physical well-being

4. **The Educational**—the opportunity to see education as an asset in dealing with tragedy

5. **The Vocational**—the alignment of my vocation and purpose

6. **The Financial**—an analysis of my finances and plans for generational wealth

7. **The Relational**—my investment in vital relationships

These "focal points" were my lifelines. When I mentioned earlier that I went through a time of dissecting, these are the areas that I had to allow God to put under His surgical knife and cut away the stuff that was causing me to drown in sorrow. I'll be the first to admit that, at times, it felt like there was no anesthesia, and I wanted to die right there on the metaphorical operating table. But, if I *had* died, then I wouldn't have such a rich and remarkable story to share with you. And while it often felt like I was being pushed closer to death than to life (sometimes with no resistance from me), I later recognized that making a committed effort to improve in every one of those areas created a strengthened connection point back to God.

An even more profound discovery, I realized that all of these focal points together created a huge window through which I could see God, and He became my main Focal Point. That's why I refer to them as Focal Points. And it's these seven Focal Points that we're going to talk about in this book.

Spiritually, we're going to discover that in times of great difficulty and hardship you either become bitter or better. This book can help to make sure you become better. We'll discuss how you become better by examining your spiritual roots, properly assessing life-changing events, and making a concerted effort to utilize the results to move out of pain and into purpose.

Soulfully, we're going to uncover the vital role that your mind, will, and emotions play in helping you navigate through tough times. I want to help you experience a breakthrough before having a break-down. We'll talk about the forces that come against your mind in times of darkness and how to combat them. We'll delve into your will and how the surrender of it creates the ultimate freedom. And we'll explore how to walk away from an emotional battlefield, wounded but wiser.

Physically, we'll examine the tremendous toll that a catastrophe can have on your physical body and how to prevent a total physical shutdown during such a crisis. We'll look at the triumph of the spirit over the physical body and how to rise to victory in the midst of physical challenges. And we'll talk about how you can be better prepared for future tough times by developing a disciplined plan for total physical fitness.

Educationally, we'll talk about how education in the midst of mind-blowing misfortune can be quite therapeutic and help put things in perspective. We'll explore the role education plays in bettering your prospects in life. And we'll talk about education as a weapon against spiritual, physical, social, and financial opposition.

Vocationally, we'll take a look at the role crises play in helping to define and refine your life's purpose. When people are faced with life-threatening situations, one of the first things they ponder is, *Am I doing what I was made to do? Do I want to spend the rest of my short time on earth doing what I'm doing right now?* I'm going to show you not only how to discover your purpose, but how to use life's difficult circumstances to catapult you right into the middle of your destiny. And we'll close this section by examining how to start where you are right now, utilizing your vocation as a means to fulfill a greater purpose in the earth.

Financially, we'll review some crucial steps you need to take in the midst of a personal crisis. We'll examine some key things you must do now, long before the winds of adversity start circulating at your doorstep. And we'll consider some ways for you to be financially proactive in your life, instead of reactive, in order to start building a generational financial legacy. And finally...

Relationally, we'll talk about relationships as an abundant source of strength during times of grief. We'll consider some vital truths you can apply to your life to reinforce your interpersonal relationships. And I'm going to show you how to develop strong, healthy relationships with the right people, and why it's so vitally important that you do it now.

It is my expectation that the examination of these seven indispensable areas of life will help you create your own "window of hope" through which you'll be able to clearly see the purposes of God articulated for your life. I believe this unique combination of my and Diane's story, the Thematic Touchpoints, and the Focal Points will work together to pull you out of darkness and into the light; out of grief and into greatness; out of sorrow and into sanity. The application of these timeless principles in my own life has manifested tremendous results, and I'm certain it will do the same for you.

WHY "BETWEEN SUNDAYS"?

Diane was born on Sunday, July 23, 1967, and she died on Sunday, January 16, 2005. It was between those two Sundays that the woman I loved more than anything lived an extraordinary, but abbreviated life.

It's *between Sundays* that you and I are faced with the monumental task of living life in a 3-D world: between the sacred, the scandalous, and the sensational.

For now, however, that's enough of the heavy stuff. It's vacation time! It's hard to find a person with more excitement and anticipation than someone who is moments away from beginning a seven-day vacation. That's the approach I want you to take when reading this book. Think of it as an all-expense paid trip to the destination of your dreams. I've already paid your way in full with the lessons I've learned as a result of my recent experiences.

That means that I'm giving you the freedom to put your worry, your guilt, and the overwhelming demands of your life on *pause* and to journey with me through this "week." Together we will discover what an amazing life we can and should all be living *between Sundays*.

SECTION I

Sunday
THE SPIRITUAL

Sunday clears away the rust of the whole week.
—JOSEPH ADDISON

Chapter 1

RISE AND SHINE

We can only appreciate the miracle of sunrise
if we have waited in the darkness.
—AUTHOR UNKNOWN

Being the first day of the week, Sunday is often associated with new beginnings or fresh starts. I think it's appropriate that we talk first about spirituality as a metaphor for Sunday because the essence of who we are originates with the spiritual, the eternal.

One of the simplest, yet most profound statements in all of Scripture is: "God is love." When I think about Diane and why I'm writing this book, I think about that love as the sun rising over the horizon on a Sunday morning. It carries on its rays divine life, love, and light to share with the world.

When discussing our spirituality and who we are by nature, I've found it most effective to observe eternal things from three perspectives. First of all, where's the beginning of our spirituality? This means both our earthly genesis (birth) and our conscious acknowledgment of a higher power from a biblical perspective (salvation), if such an acknowledgment has been made.

Second, when and what was the last life-changing event that caused us to reevaluate our spirituality?

And third, how did that life-changing event affect our spirituality, both inwardly and outwardly, going forward?

By examining these three perspectives on spirituality, it becomes much easier to put together a solution-oriented plan that not only prepares us for Monday, but also empowers the rest of our "week." There's nothing quite like starting off our week with a renewed spiritual perspective, one that will ensure good success for its duration, despite the unexpected setbacks that will arise.

Chapter 2

BEATINGS AND BIRTHING IN MISSISSIPPI

Human beings are not born once and for all on the day their mothers give birth to them, but...life obliges them over and over again to give birth to themselves.

—GABRIEL GARCIA MARQUEZ

For Diane, it all began one Sunday in July 1967, in a tiny town down South. It's highly unlikely you've ever heard of Winona, Mississippi. In fact, most people in the late 1960s hadn't heard of Winona either, until an incident a few years before Diane's birth put it on the map and seared the city into the collective conscience of America. Winona is one of those towns that if you glance down and reach for your map while driving through, you'll find yourself lost in Duck Hill, the next town over. The nation's population has ballooned to 300 million people, yet only 5,482 of them reside in Winona. Even today you can still buy a house in Winona for about $25,000, and rent one for about $350.

LIFE BETWEEN SUNDAYS

The city is probably best known as the place where, in 1963, civil rights leader and activist Fannie Lou Hamer was savagely and unjustly beaten by several police officers. Hamer was passing through Winona on her way to organizing Mississippi's "Freedom Summer" as a means of combating the racial oppression and injustices of the era. As a contemporary of Dr. Martin Luther King Jr., Hamer was working on behalf of the Student Nonviolent Coordinating Committee (SNCC) when she and a few colleagues unceremoniously stopped in a Winona diner for a quick meal one humid afternoon in June.

Unhappy with where Hamer had been, and even more disgusted by where she was headed, some of Winona's racist police officers took matters into their own hands. They determined to introduce Hamer to some Southern street justice. For Hamer, dessert ended up being a cold serving of false accusations heaped over jail time, and a bludgeoning so gruesome it would take months for her to recover. And she never fully recovered.

In the end, Hamer served as a beautiful illustration of someone who became better when faced with horrendous circumstances. That incident in Winona only fueled Hamer's fire, causing her to become even more outspoken for equality and emboldening her stance against the racial injustices of the day. She went on to become a civil rights pioneer, known for her plain-spoken manner and her fervent belief in the biblical righteousness of her cause. Here's an excerpt from a book about Hamer to provide a little insight into her determined personality.

> In Ruleville, the selective boycott began when Hamer accompanied a group of blacks to the mayor's office to request the firing of a policeman who shot a young black man, Paul Jackson, for no apparent reason...it was at that point that an incensed Hamer and other citizens decided to quit buying in Ruleville stores. During the campaign Hamer noted that the boycott had been "98 percent effective." With indignation, she observed in her signature style: "Some of the store-

keepers complain they may go out of business; well, we've been out of business all the time!…The white man around here don't realize how good it would be to let us up out of the ditch. He can't keep us in the ditch without standing on us, and he can't get out of the ditch without letting us out."[1]

Regardless of the family you were born into, or the circumstances surrounding your birth, God had foreknowledge of your arrival long before your conception. There's victory in knowing that your birth was not accidental, and that you have a specific purpose to fulfill during your lifetime.

While Hamer's attack was an unfortunate blemish on an otherwise quaint town, she must have left some residue of her fiery and determined spirit there because Winona would again make the history books, at least my personal history book, just over four years later. On July 23, 1967, Annie B. Greer gave birth to Diane Nevette Greer, my future bride and a trailblazer in her own right. Diane's birth didn't draw quite the same crowds and national press attention as the Hamer ruckus, but I'm convinced that there was some sort of stirring along Winona's dusty roads on that humid Sunday morning.

I also believe that there was the same sort of stirring when you were born. A specific purpose was conceived in your mother's womb; God wrapped flesh around that purpose; and several months later the world was introduced to a unique new brand called "you." It's important to know that like Diane's humble beginnings in Winona, Mississippi, we all have a place of origin; a place we can look back to and say, "That's where it all began!"

The Bible has this to say:

Before I formed you in the womb I knew you, before you were born I set you apart; I appointed you as a prophet to the nations (Jeremiah 1:5).

Where you are today is a collective of distinct experiences you've had between then and now and how you've responded to those experiences. If you sat down and took an inventory of your life, you could probably recount at least one or two experiences that rattled you to your core and caused you to look inwardly. I believe that God has built a mechanism into our spiritual DNA that, irrespective of where we are in our spiritual journey, causes us to instinctively start asking spiritual questions when life turns sour.

Take a moment and reflect on your own earthly start. Go on the Internet and do a search of the day you were born. You'll be surprised at all of the events that took place on the day you took your first breath outside of the womb. You are a part of that history, and that makes you special. Whether or not you made the headlines, you're significant.

When I looked up my own date of birth, I was intrigued to discover that while my mother was giving birth to me in Shreveport, Louisiana, the United States was signing an agreement with China to loan the country a shipping vessel, the *U.S.S. Yarnall*. On the same day, the song "Mrs. Robinson" by Simon and Garfunkel hit Number One on the Billboard Charts.

When I looked up Diane's date of birth, I discovered that 43 people died in a race riot in Detroit, in what's historically become known as Detroit's 12th Street Riot, one of the worst riots in U.S. history. The riot caused the city of Detroit and the entire nation to begin seriously rethinking the unfair lending and hiring practices and widespread discrimination that had plagued the city for decades.

The day you were born is also important, if for no other reason than the fact that you arrived that day, bringing a smile to God's face and joy to someone's life. Regardless of the day of the week on which you were born, on your date of birth you represented somebody's "Sunday Morning"—a fresh start, full of wonder and possibilities.

The same can be said of any day in your life when you have an authentic spiritual encounter with God; a time when you know God is speaking to your heart. Despite what's going on in your life at the time, when you have one of those spiritual encounters where God reveals Himself to you like never before, it once again becomes an opportunity to start afresh, a chance to make sure the rest of your life counts for something.

This quote, from a book I read recently, says it best:

> Perhaps no place echoes with eternity quite like a cemetery.... Looking at old tombstones, I can't help but recognize that entire lives are now reduced before me to two dates and one little dash. Some monuments include facts or sayings, Bible verses or poignant memorials, but each person's life really comes down to what transpired between those two dates. It comes down to what's in the dash. I look at the dash of a particular person's marker and wonder, *What did he live for? Whom did she love? What were his passions? What were her biggest mistakes and greatest regrets?*[2]

ENDNOTES

1. Chana Kai Lee, *For Freedom's Sake: The Life of Fannie Lou Hamer* (Chicago: University of Illinois Press, 1999).

2. Kerry and Chris Shook, *One Month to Live* (Colorado Springs: Waterbrook, 2008).

Chapter 3

CLOSE ENCOUNTERS OF THE GOD KIND

> There is no object that we see; no action that we
> do; no good that we enjoy; no evil that we feel, or
> fear, but we may make some spiritual advantage of
> all: and he that makes such improvement is wise, as
> well as pious.
>
> —ANNE BRADSTREET

I don't know the exact date when Diane had her first spiritual encounter, but I do know that on her way to it she asked lots of questions. An inquisitive person by nature, Diane was the type of kid who was always on a search for truth and meaning. From grade school on, Diane demonstrated a tremendous aptitude for all things science. One of the things she often pondered was why she and her siblings had coarse or "nappy" hair while her parents and grandparents had fine, straight hair. I don't think Diane got a satisfactory answer until many years later when she enrolled at Tougaloo University and took a course on genetics. Even after her discovery, I think she still carried a little good-natured resentment for not getting those "good hair" genes.

Diane won many awards for science throughout junior high and high school, the most memorable being a Bausch & Lomb Science Award she won her senior year of high school. I'm convinced that Diane approached her spirituality with the same type of analytical interrogation. At some point, Diane's keen intellect collided with a real and living God, lighting her heart and turning honest skepticism into passionate faith. You can probably recall times in your life when you've experienced similar collisions between the analytical equations you've come up with to explain life and God's divine decimal point.

You've probably heard the saying, "I can't see the forest for all the trees." Truth is something that can be revealed to you when and where you least expect it, right in the middle of your situation. Look for Truth in your current circumstances, and think of ways the application of it could be the solution you've been searching for.

Having experienced tragedy very early in life, Diane had good reason to be a skeptic. When Diane was still a child, her mother had a fifth baby, a girl they named Doris Elaine. This new baby girl was the tiebreaker! Diane had two brothers and one sister, so the birth of Doris Elaine meant that the girls had won. They finally outnumbered the boys. The whole family rejoiced the day Doris Elaine was born. That day was full of enough laughter, tears of joy, strategizing (world domination for the girls), and plans for Doris Elaine's future to fill a manuscript.

Twenty-four hours later, however, little Doris Elaine lay dead in her hospital crib, and all the hopes and aspirations with her. While it was undoubtedly one of the saddest days for the entire family, what Diane and her sister, Dalre, remembered most vividly is how they had packed a lifetime worth of dreams into that 24-hour period. One event like that could have very easily been more than a young girl could bear, but that wasn't the end of the family tragedies.

Diane's father abandoned the family for good just after her ninth birthday, and it had a tremendous impact on their home. Diane and her siblings suddenly lost one of their emotional anchors, and it was overwhelming and traumatizing. I think her parent's separation was one of the things that caused Diane to be so introspective and rigorous in thought. For the first time in her life she was experiencing the thornier side of human existence: tough questions with answers that made you gulp; only this gulp felt like swallowing a cactus. *How could Daddy just up and leave us like that? There has to be an answer for this!* she thought. Spoken like a true scientist.

Like all of us, Diane learned that some questions are like cul-de-sacs: circular with the only exit putting you right back where you started—still determined, but frustrated. But that didn't stop Diane from asking. More importantly, it didn't stop Diane from eventually finding Truth, or, to be more precise, Truth finding her.

How do you find Truth or be found by Truth? Sometimes Truth finds you where you least expect it, right in the middle of a storm.

Chapter 4

NO TIME FOR NAPPING

My sense is that planned, permitted, endorsed napping by management is still rare.

—DAVID DINGES

Have you ever been just about ready to lie down for a nice, tranquil Sunday afternoon nap when something happens that not only ruins your nap, but transforms the rest of the week's forecast from *sunny with light breezes* to *stormy with severe tornado warnings?* I experienced such an interruption when I learned the full extent of Diane's illness. I don't think I could rearticulate it any better than one of my journal entries from soon after receiving the news.

 Sunday, June 15, 2003:
The Day of Diane's Diagnosis

Today was a day of great expectations. Diane and I had longed to discover what had ailed her for several years. With her consistent stomach pains, we thought maybe she had a very serious case of acid reflux. She knew going in for the biopsy that they would discover the culprit, but neither of us could have predicted the outcome. She had already gone through a series of other tests, including a test for brain cancer, so this was the big one. They wanted to biopsy her liver. It wasn't a long procedure, but sitting there in the waiting room, it felt like the seasons going from spring to winter. I sat there quietly waiting for it to be over. I prayed and negotiated with God for things to be well. When you are in a place like that, it causes you to lay it all on the altar. It was like Hannah when she wanted a child so badly that she was willing to lay it all on the altar. In that moment, Hannah's story brought a small morsel of comfort to my restless heart.

> *In bitterness of soul Hannah wept much and prayed to the Lord. And she made a vow, saying, "O Lord Almighty, if You will only look upon Your servant's misery and remember me, and not forget Your servant but give her a son, then I will give him to the Lord for all the days of his life, and no razor will ever be used on his head"* (1 Samuel 1:10-11).

As I meditated on that verse, I thought about how at one point during her petition, Hannah refers to herself in the third person, "Lord, if You will only look upon *Your servant....*" It was as if the pain was so intense in that moment that she couldn't even bear to ask for help in the first person. That's how I felt in that waiting room, "Lord, if You will just not forget Your servant Joseph concerning this circumstance...." I just wanted Diane to be OK.

Honestly, there was such a silence in my spirit that I wondered if God heard me that day. The truth is that, in that moment, I wasn't ready to deal with God's answer. Isaiah 55:8 declares that His ways are not our ways and His thoughts are not our thoughts. Here I am writing a journal entry and already a sermon is coming out. I guess a preacher can't stop being a preacher. I feel like I'm coming face to face with the sovereignty of God.

After an hour or so, the doctor darkened the doorway of the waiting room. I never shall forget that look on his face. I think the darkness came more from the expression on his face than from his blocking any actual light from the hallway. You know that look. That stare that forewarns, "I've got something I'm about to tell you; you're not going to like it, and I really wish I wasn't the bearer of this news. In fact, you'd better sit down first."

I braced myself as he clasped his sweaty hands. When he spoke it was as if his mouth was moving in slow motion. It sounded like someone playing a recording of Darth Vader's voice backward.

"We found tumors on your wife's pancreas and liver."

But what I heard sounded like Charlie Brown's teacher calling, "WAH WA WA WAH WAH!"

And just like that, my world turned upside down. Actually, "upside down" is too polite. My world collapsed into a pool of morbid shock right there on that icy linoleum floor.

"It's neuroendocrine pancreatic cancer."

Before I even understood the full ramifications of the diagnosis, hearing the title alone sent chills down my spine. The fact that it had spread to her liver was an indication that we were already in Stage 4, which usually greatly reduces one's life expectancy.

I sat there numb, trying to figure out what Scriptures I could bring to remembrance, yet I was strangled by the overwhelming emotions of the moment. I had counseled people for years on how to respond when the physician gives you bad news, but in that moment I began to realize that there are times when taking your own medicine can be frightening, traumatic, and downright disgusting.

After the shock came fear, and after fear—anger. I knew then that my spiritual resolve had to go to another place. I immediately walked into the hallway and talked to God. I'm sure people saw me and thought I had lost my mind. But when you enter into a place of warfare like that, you lose sight of your surroundings. I needed to talk to God, and I needed Him to know right then that I needed Him more than ever before. Feelings of extreme loneliness and trepidation bombarded me in that moment. Even with being the pastor of a church with more than 20,000 members, and having the incredible circle of friends I'm blessed to have, I shuffled through that hallway by myself, like crawling through a thorny brier garden—bruised and alone.

I knew that I still had the gargantuan task of discussing the test results with Diane after the anesthesia dissipated. The surgeon told me to wait before I informed her, and I did. Once again, it felt like the seasons changed. Diane was still heavily medicated when we left the hospital that day, so it wasn't the appropriate time to share the news. We drove home together, both in a heavily dazed fog, hers induced by medicine, mine by horror.

When we arrived home, I held Diane like I never had before. Even in Diane's groggy state, I'm sure she could sense in my touch that I was holding and rocking her in near desperation, my stomach increasingly knotting up with each sway back and forth. She fell right asleep. I cried.

Later that night, we were talking, and she wanted to know the outcome of the tests. I told her that we were scheduled to go back at noon the next day to meet with the surgeon, but that was not a satisfactory answer. In that moment, I felt a kindred spirit with the doctor because I then knew exactly how he was feeling when he had to share the news with me and how difficult it must have been for him. Sharing the diagnosis with Diane was made all the more difficult by the fact that, while she lay sleeping, I researched the form of cancer with which she was diagnosed. Based on the stage of her cancer, I kept seeing life expectancies that never exceeded five years. That ripped my heart out. All I could think about were the lively discussions we'd had about kids and grandkids. The disintegration of those dreams brought on a bitter chill as they reflected off the cold, hard facts written on my computer screen.

Diane put those eyes on me, and she knew I was butter when she did that. She could get her way like that. When she prodded for the full report, I shakily repeated what the doctor had shared with me, and she actually said she was relieved.

My mouth opened up like the Grand Canyon. I said, "What?"

With utter simplicity and quiet faith, Diane told me that she just wanted to know because she had grown weary of the tests over the years. Now she knew what she was fighting. What a woman of faith! Here I was, a man of God, esteemed pastor of one of the largest churches in the country, trembling in my voice and knock-kneed to share such devastating news, and Diane was sitting straight up with godly confidence saying, "I know what I'm fighting now."

Right then, I knew that this woman's faith was not some public façade. It was a real and living faith. It was on that day, and in that instant, we knew our faith had to join like never before to fight an enemy we then knew by name, "neuroendocrine pancreatic cancer."

If you want me to be brutally honest about the first thing that came to my mind, I can only describe it as a question that ends with symbols, "What the $&!@?" I never knew so many four-letter words could run through one's mind in such rapid succession. In my own defense, my spirit man did simultaneously kick into gear, and I began to pray.

If you've ever had the solemn responsibility to be either the bearer or recipient of bad news, then you're well acquainted with the eerie stillness that enters the room just before the announcement. It's like you could hear a single pin drop, but at the same time, you'd swear a thousand pins were stabbing you all over your body, and the pain adds to the deafening. And I'm not talking about news like your dog died or your empty house burned down. Not to diminish those types of tragedies, but I'm talking about the kind of news that causes all the color in your body to run to a corner and hide, forcing your body into a ghost-like state. I mean the kind of news that even if you're sitting when you receive it, your knees still buckle and knock together, and your body instinctively starts curving into the fetal position.

The doctor did his best to put a positive spin on things and make me feel at ease. Unfortunately, no matter how clever your delivery, the sentence, "You're wife has inoperable Stage 4 pancreatic cancer," comes at you like a full arsenal of verbal bullets at point-blank range. It was the kind of news that makes the word "blindsided" sound like a nursery rhyme title. It really was akin to an out-of-body moment.

I can still see myself sitting in front of the doctor stoically nodding, his words slowly morphing into that Darth Vader recording. There I sat, Dr. Bishop Joseph Warren Walker III, standing strong by his beloved, drinking in the news like a seasoned spiritual warrior. Truth be told, at that moment in my mind's eye, I was Baby Joe. I was frantically crawling in circles on that cold, raw, waiting room floor, drowning in my own tears, desperately searching for someone to pick me up and hold me.

Looking back, I'm convinced it was a quickening of the Spirit of God that allowed me to pull it together and instantly determine that Diane and I would not surrender without a spiritual fight to the better end.

Chapter 5

FINDING CHEMO

During chemo, you're more tired than you've ever been. It's like a cloud passing over the sun, and suddenly you're out. You don't know how you'll answer the door when your groceries are delivered. But you also find that you're stronger than you've ever been. You're clear. Your mortality is at optimal distance, not up so close that it obscures everything else, but close enough to give you depth perception. Previously, it has taken you weeks, months, or years to discover the meaning of an experience. Now it's instantaneous.

—MELISSA BANK

I don't know if you've ever been to a chemotherapy session, but if you haven't, trust me when I say that it's one of those things that is painful to read about, let alone experience firsthand. Just weeks after Diane's diagnosis I was spending Sundays preaching to multitudes and watching God do great things in the lives of His people, and then just two days later, I was watching the doctor shoot a chemical warfare agent through my wife's veins. I was feeling about as helpless as a crippled child. My mind wasn't even functioning right, but Diane was taking it in stride.

I was the man who had been able to help so many people through crisis situations, but now that I was facing my own, I didn't know if I'd make it through. I literally had to put my emotional state on autopilot just so I could keep showing up and ministering to the congregation. Otherwise, I would have been a blubbering mess in the pulpit.

Before long, I was going to chemo sessions where so many of Diane's veins had been burned out by the radiation treatment that it would take the nurse 30 minutes to find a viable one. I found myself preparing lessons on hope and faith while my own life appeared to be in a state of hopeless dismay.

It was at this point that I had to make a conscious determination of which road I would travel. I did find some comfort in the eloquent words of Brennan Manning.

> The denial of death is not a healthy option for a disciple of Christ. Nor is pessimism in the face of today's troubles. The significant shift in priorities that comes through living twenty-four hours at a time is not mere resignation to what we know cannot be changed. My life in the confrontation with trials and tribulations is not stoic passivity. My death-defying "no" to despair at the end of my life and my life-affirming "yes" to seemingly insurmountable problems in the midst of my life are both animated by hope in the invincible might of the risen Jesus Christ and in "the immeasurable scope of His power in us who believe" (Ephesians 1:19).[1]

ENDNOTE

1. Brennan Manning, *The Rabbi's Heartbeat* (Colorado Springs: NavPress, 2003).

Chapter 6

BITTER OR BETTER

Reflect upon your present blessings, of which every man has many—not on your past misfortunes, of which all men have some.

—CHARLES DICKENS

Do your trials make you *bitter* or *better?* That's the $64,000 question when discussing your spiritual growth in the midst of insurmountable troubles. That was the question I was asking myself as I wrote in my journal. I'll also be the first to admit that when the doctor told me Diane had cancer, I was dancing back and forth between that "i" and "e," still fighting an intense internal battle, and still not knowing if I was going to become *bitter* or get *better.* At one time or another, each of us has come to this crossroads in our own lives, or we have watched someone else approach this inescapable fork in life's road.

I'm sure you've known or read about a mother who loses a child to drunk driving and then goes on to become a crusader for Mothers Against Drunk Driving (MADD), giving passionate speeches, sharing valuable information with teens, and bettering lives in the process. I know that I've become passionate about some causes because of past traumatic experiences. I started a program at my church to send buses to area colleges every Sunday to pick up students who wanted to attend church, feed them a hot meal, and then deliver them safely back to campus. The inspiration for that program was born, partly, out of my experiences with an overt anti-God stance at three different secular universities I attended. Something was ignited within me to at least provide students with an opportunity to hear an alternate point of view from what their professors were force-feeding them in class all week.

There's no doubt that there are going to be things that happen in your life that make you feel like you've been delivered the knock-out blow. Sometimes it's almost easier to want to bleed to death on the mat; but there are people sitting ringside who need you, people expecting you to get up and go another round. For their sake and yours, get up!

On the other hand, you've probably also known someone who, after an unexpected tragedy, allowed their anger to take them down a long road of bitterness and resentment. In the end, that person not only ruined their own life, but they often left a destructive trail of poisonous regret in the lives of those they encountered. Having been in the ministry for almost 20 years now, I know far too many pastors who abused their ministerial office and consequently lost many of their congregants. But instead of working toward restoration and repentance, they became bitter and began to poison the lives of remaining members rather than speaking life to the multitudes.

I'm convinced that life is a series of tests that all have the same two multiple-choice answers: bitter or better. Some events cause a slight nudge in one direction or the other, while others feel like a hard shove from a belligerent bully. It's this latter kind of shove that I experienced when Diane became ill. Although it felt like that bully called "life" blindsided me with a knockout punch, I knew I couldn't stay down for the "10" count. And *you* can't stay down on the mat either.

As the moon chased the sun into Monday on that bleak Sunday night, I committed to do some things spiritually, knowing Monday was going to be all out warfare on my mind, will, and emotions. For the first time in my life, I had serious doubts as to whether or not I was going to be able to apply the same faith and principles that I had been preaching to people, Sunday after Sunday for more than a decade, to my own tragic circumstances. That petrifying doubt literally forced me to sit down with pen in hand, hot tears smearing the ink, and sketch out some "Spiritual Lifelines." I knew that I was already on the verge of putting my Christianity on pause (as foolish as that sounds). I needed practical solutions to prevent me from doing so. I believe applying these "spiritual lifelines" to whatever difficulties you may now be facing will bring comfort, hope, and the spiritual empowerment you need to go on.

Spiritual Lifelines for Your Spirit

1. When faced with a tragic circumstance, look to God as part of the solution, not the cause of the problem. As bad as I wanted to blame God when Diane became ill, deep down I knew it was not

His fault. I knew that in the long run it was going to be much more productive for me to be on the offense alongside God (allowing Him to be the solution for healing), not on the defense (bitterly blaming Him for my pain and cursing His name).

2. Surround yourself with people who've experienced what you're dealing with. There's kinship and healing in fellowshipping with others who can authentically and empathetically relate to your circumstances.

3. Don't shut down your life's routine. While it's appropriate to take time to heal from a tragedy, you'll find tremendous strength (though difficult at first) in continuing on with your job, raising your kids, or whatever your life's routine may entail.

4. Spend more time with God than ever before. Immediately after a tragedy, things like watching television and just hanging out become meaningless. Utilize that "meaningless space" to allow God to pour life back into your spirit through prayer, Bible study, and worship.

Applying these Spiritual Lifelines to your life won't necessarily mean that Sunday night won't be dark, but it will mean that you'll go into Monday morning with the attitude that everything in life is seasonal, with change always on the horizon.

SECTION II

Monday
THE SOULFUL

On Monday, when the sun is hot,
I wonder to myself a lot
Now is it true, or is it not
That what is which and which is what?

—A.A. HODGES

Chapter 7

DAZED AND CONFUSED

The door is probably what saved her. It would have
protected her from the debris. She crawled up out of
the rubble. A paramedic found her wandering around
in a daze.

—JOHN OXENDINE

I t's easy to wake up on a Monday morning in a state of bewilder-
ment. Depending on what your weekend was like, you're either
wishing it was Saturday morning again, or you're projecting yourself
into next weekend, hoping for a better outcome. Literally and figura-
tively speaking, the *soul* can often be a little foggy come Monday
morning.

With all of the intricacies of being human, it's very difficult to
come up with a precise definition for the soul. Nevertheless, philosophers and theologians have, throughout the centuries, come to somewhat of a general consensus that the soul can be defined as a person's
mind, will, and emotions. The *mind* serves as the seat of your creative,
analytical, and intellectual activity; the *will* is your cognitive ability to

make choices; and the *emotions* serve as your physical response to living, both the inward and outward. It's as if your soul acts as a fair-weather friend to your spirit and your body, cozying up to one or the other, depending on which one gives it the most affection.

For most of us, come early Monday morning, the soul is usually getting a little more comfortable with the physical aspect of your being; telling you to sleep in a little longer, and supplying unhealthy doses of dread and anxiety with respect to the week ahead. This is usually the root cause of not even wanting to get out of bed.

You can probably imagine that with the kind of Sunday night I just described having, my outlook Monday morning was bleak at best. At least that's what the facts said. I'm talking about one of those Monday mornings when the weather's been forecasted as *strong winds, heavy rains, and hail* for the foreseeable future. More than just *hail* pelting me from the sky, I had the forces of *hell* bombarding my soul.

You've doubtless heard the saying, "Practice what you preach." This was a time when I had to live that saying like never before. I can literally think of hundreds of people who've come to me for counsel and wisdom regarding unimaginable circumstances, and my counsel has always included the overarching theme that God is going to "work it out." Fortunately, regardless of how bad those situations were, I did always see God work it out. It wasn't always in the exact way that any of us expected, but He did, nonetheless, work it out.

I was clinging by a thread to that small nugget of truth that I'd experienced both first- and secondhand. But it would be unfair to start this Monday off on such a dreary note—attempting to share with you how to protect your soul in a crisis—without going back a couple of days to Saturday and sharing some memories that brought some hazy sunshine to an otherwise depressingly gray, Monday morning.

Chapter 8

SERMONS OVER SANDWICHES

No, this trick won't work.... How on earth are you
ever going to explain in terms of chemistry and physics
so important a biological phenomenon as first love?
—ALBERT EINSTEIN

I met Diane at an Omega Phi Psi fraternity party one Saturday
night while she was a student at Meharry Dental School and I was
working on my Masters of Divinity at Vanderbilt. Since I was going
to school full-time, coupled with working as an associate pastor at my
church, those Saturday parties were really my only opportunity to
socialize and unwind. I didn't drink or smoke, but I did have a great
time dancing, conversing, and meeting lots of interesting new people.

It was the early 1990s, a time when the United States was entering
a decade of vast optimism, and I felt like my prospects for a successful
life were looking pretty good too. I sensed great things were in my
future, and spotting Diane at the party that night only reinforced that
sense of hopefulness. I watched Diane from a distance that night,
waiting for the opportune moment to approach her. Somehow I ended

up right in front of the table where she was sitting with a friend.

I already knew Diane because I had spotted her at church one Sunday, and she stood out from the crowd. (Nashville is one of those towns where it's easy to run into the same person on repeat occasions, especially amongst college students.) At church, I had roused enough courage to at least say hello, but she left service before I had a chance to meet her.

I don't want to step on any "religious toes," but it is OK to have a good time in life. I don't mean being excessive, or doing things that can damage your spirit, mind, and body, but it is acceptable to experience fun and fellowship in life. There's really no other way to create fond memories than by enjoying life. There will come a time when you'll want to recount some of those occasions.

Diane remembered me too. After a few minutes of light banter, it was either time for me to politely fade back into the party, or walk away with a phone number in my hand. When we reached the apex of that uncomfortable moment, Diane's friend gave her a look like, "Do you want me to have a pen?"

I still don't know how Diane communicated to her friend to

produce the pen (I'm sure it was some sort of nonverbal glance that only best friends understand), but I thank God for that secret communication. We exchanged numbers that night, and it wasn't long before we were hanging out all the time.

I was on my way to being a pastor, and Diane was finishing up her dental studies. Our first date was a meal of pork-n-beans that I cooked in my little beat-up "itchen." (It wasn't even big enough to call it a kitchen.) That's how poor we were going through school. After our meal, we sat on my "pleather" couch and talked for hours. I say "pleather" because that's all I owned, a secondhand, plastic-leather couch. I don't even think my wallet was leather, not that I had money to fill it anyway.

One thing I remember distinctly is being able to sit and talk to Diane for hours. I guess that's one positive thing about being a starving student: you can't afford to be a club-hopper and spend your nights out on the town, so you just plop down on a couch, with a warmed-over can of beans, and chat the night away.

Now I know that people do other things on couches too, but Diane and I were nerds. We'd sit there and debate about the global economy and politics, or philosophize about potential solutions for making the world a better place. I believe some of the content for my early sermons was born out of those thought-provoking conversations with Diane. One thing I know for certain is that my growing affection for Diane was birthed in those times of innocent communion.

Chapter 9

BACK TO REALITY

Once the job is done, then it will be time to look back
and reminisce. But right now, there is still a job to do.
—NATE WHITFORD

Reminiscing in my mind about the time and place I met Diane
was one of the things that helped me stay sane after getting the
news of her illness. That's one of the beautiful things about the mind:
when the pain of the present becomes overbearing, your mind can
travel to a happier time to ease the pain.

The last time you experienced a difficult time in your life, or if you're
in the middle of one now, you know all too well that while your mind is
consumed with grief, life doesn't stop going on around you. You still have
a job, bills, kids, and other responsibilities to attend to. It's often those
hectic responsibilities, coupled with the grief you're experiencing from a
traumatic circumstance, that can make your mind start to meltdown.
That's the sort of reality I was living with when Diane became ill.

As the senior pastor of a church with three separate locations around
the city of Nashville, I couldn't just put life on pause. To top it off, when

Diane was diagnosed, the church was right in the middle of a $17-million-dollar building and development project! Saying I had a lot on my mind would be a gross understatement. My Sundays and Wednesdays were usually typified by delivering a message of encouragement and hope no less than six times—hardly days to unwind and chill out.

Between Sundays, then and now, you'll most likely find me traveling the globe sharing the message of God's truth or dealing with the issues and inevitable "fires" commonly associated with leading a megachurch and overseeing several business and nonprofit organizations. I don't share my responsibilities to boast, but only to allow you to peer inside my mind and get a glimpse of the crushing responsibilities I had to maintain, while my mind was also working overtime processing an overwhelming loss.

There's absolutely nothing wrong with reminiscing about good times you've experienced in your life. It's OK to think back on happier times as a reminder that life is seasonal, which means that regardless of present circumstances, joyous times will come again.

Believe me, I would have traded it all at a moment's notice to be back on that "pleather" couch, eating cold beans with a healthy, vibrant Diane.

Regardless of what any given week holds for me, I make it a point to be back at my post on Sunday, delivering a message of encouragement and hope to God's people. That means that whether I've had a week of peaks or valleys, or both, is completely irrelevant. Sunday after Sunday, irrespective of what happens in between, I have a responsibility to stand before God's people in love and deliver a word of truth.

I share this point simply as a statement of fact, not an admission of a burden. I love my congregation, and I love what I do! But believe me, Sunday keeps coming, and my mind began to struggle with the magnitude of it all soon after Diane's diagnosis. It sometimes felt like my mind was sliding off an embankment into a mental cesspool of fear, despair, and guilt. Here's another journal entry to prove my point.

Monday, June 23, 2003: Mind Games

Diane has such an aggressive form of cancer that we were back at the hospital for more tests. This place is beginning to feel a little too familiar. It reminds me of my days as a young pastor visiting sick members. Even then, I always felt unsettled as soon as those huge glass doors closed behind me, and a long, sterile, concrete, and brightly lit linoleum corridor lay ahead. I've often wondered if they make those lights so bright to somehow give people a feeling of sunshine because the hospital can be a dreary place.

I thought back today to when I was studying for my Masters at Vanderbilt. As a part of my Clinical Pastoral Education (CPE), I spent an extended amount of time serving at Our Lady of the Lake Regional Medical Center in Baton Rouge, Louisiana. What I distinctly remember is that I was stationed on the Oncology Floor of the hospital, spiritually attending to cancer patients. Thinking back on it now, I believe God was preparing me for days like today.

I'm glad Diane's sister, Dalre, was with us today. At least on this visit, we split the trepidation in thirds instead of just in half. Maybe we need to start making these hospital visits in groups of five or more. That way it won't be so painful.

At the conclusion of our appointment with the oncologist, instead of sending us home, he sent us upstairs. Today I figured out that it's not a good sign when the doctor is sending you upstairs, rather than stamping your parking ticket and sending you home.

It almost seemed as if the higher the floor, the more serious your condition. I'm dreading the day that they tell us we need to visit the penthouse. I almost feel like going up there would put us one floor away from eternity. I also noticed that a lot of these hospitals and medical buildings don't have a 13th floor. Maybe that's the floor that leads to Judgment, and the button only appears in the elevator when it's your turn to get off on that floor.

As soon as the doctor instructed us to go up instead of down, that's when the guilt hit my mind like a freight train. I'm scheduled to preach tonight in another city....

I had been hoping that after we saw the oncologist I'd get to spend some quiet time at home with Diane before my trip. The doctor telling us we needed to go upstairs ruined my plans, and threw me for a loop. This whole cancer thing in general has shattered my plans. My long-term plans have been reduced to the life span of a AAA battery (about 6 months), and now my short-term plans can't catch a break either.

Diane played the role of strong woman today. She assured me that everything was fine, and that I should proceed as planned. She reassured me that with Dalre being there, she had the support she needed.

Although we got in the elevator together, Diane went upstairs to see another cancer specialist, and I got my parking ticket stamped and flew out of Nashville for a preaching engagement. It's going to be difficult to preach tonight with my mind in this state of flux. Maybe that's what I need to preach about.

When you have times in your life that your mind is telling you one thing and your spirit another, go with your spirit. When circumstances are overwhelming, your mind wants to run and find relief, while your spirit wants to stay, fight, and work through the pain. Work through it, and you'll have fewer regrets.

I later learned that Diane was really scared that day and was hoping deep down that I would cancel my preaching engagement and stay with her. Talk about having your mind flooded with guilt and regret!

PERCEPTION ABOUT DECEPTION

You don't get to choose how you are going to die or
when. You can only decide how you're going to live.
—JOAN BAEZ

Several years ago, a rap group called "The Ghetto Boys" had a hit
song entitled "My Mind's Playing Tricks on Me." In that song,
they humorously chronicle how the pressures of life can cause your
mind to start playing tricks on you. I think the song, and more importantly, its title are fitting as we transition into talking about the second
aspect of your soul: your will.

"If you think you cannot be deceived, you already have been."
Diane spoke those words at a women's conference in 2003. Diane was
always very intuitive and discerning, yet she never allowed herself to be
fooled into thinking that she could never be deceived. She was always
on guard for deception creeping into her own life and the lives of those
around her.

After Diane was diagnosed with cancer, she refused to be deceived
into thinking she had to just give up and die. I believe that's one of the

reasons she survived as long as she did with a form of cancer that's been known to kill many in a matter of weeks or even days.

In order to live a victorious life, it's important for you to have a healthy respect for deception. Deception, like sin, is always waiting patiently at the door of your heart for the opportune time to take center stage. But your life can be deception-free as long as you remember those wonderful words of wisdom: "If you think you cannot be deceived, you already have been."

Diane was able to keep her mind from playing tricks on her because from the outset of her diagnosis, she made a conscious decision to surrender her will in exchange for whatever outcome God had already determined. That did not mean that she wasn't ready to put up a fight. Fight she did. She fought knowing that the Bible commanded her to do so, but she realized that the ultimate victory was in knowing God had already worked it out. In fact, Diane and I both agreed that complete trust and a total surrender of our wills to God was the only way that we could possibly endure.

An entry from the timeless classic *My Utmost for His Highest* says it best:

WILL YOU GO OUT WITHOUT KNOWING

"He went out, not knowing whither he went."
Hebrews 11:8

Have you been "out" in this way? If so, there is no logical statement possible when anyone asks you what you are doing. One of the difficulties in Christian work is this question—"What do you expect to do?" You do not know what you are going to do; the only thing you know is that God knows what He is doing. Continually revise your attitude toward God and see if it is a going out of everything, trusting in God entirely. It is this attitude that keeps you in perpetual wonder—you do not know what God is going to do next. Each morning you wake it is to be a "going out," building in confidence on God. "Take no thought for your life, . . . nor yet for your body"—take no thought for the things for which you did take thought before you "went out."

Have you been asking God what He is going to do? He will never tell you. God does not tell you what He is going to do; He reveals to you who He is. Do you believe in a miracle-working God, and will you go out in surrender to Him until you are not surprised an atom at anything He does?

Suppose God is the God you know Him to be when you are nearest to Him—what an impertinence worry is! Let the attitude of the life be a continual "going out" in dependence upon God, and your life will have an ineffable charm about it which is a satisfaction to Jesus. You have to learn to go out of convictions, out of creeds, out of experiences, until so far as your faith is concerned, there is nothing between yourself and God.[1]

ENDNOTE

1. Oswald Chambers, *My Utmost for His Highest* (Westwood, NJ: Barbour, 1935), January 2.

Chapter 11

DUELING IN THE DARK

> The marvelous richness of human experience would
> lose something of rewarding joy if there were no
> limitations to overcome. The hilltop hour would
> not be half so wonderful if there were no dark
> valleys to traverse.
>
> —HELEN KELLER

The days and weeks immediately following the diagnosis were some of the most difficult because Diane had just started chemotherapy, and we were both utilizing every ounce of faith and energy to resist succumbing to fear. We were trying our hardest to "revise our attitudes...trusting in God entirely," as the devotional from *My Utmost for His Highest* advised.

I can count on one finger the number of nights of full sleep I got during those early weeks. And the one night I did sleep well was purely a result of my body completely shutting down from fatigue and exhaustion. One particular night I didn't sleep at all. I thought my mind was playing tricks on me. As I lay there wide-eyed in the dark, I saw these black shadows darting across the room. I had to rub my eyes to make sure I was really awake. As soon as I stopped rubbing I felt a strange suffocation, and a murderous voice shouted, "I'm going to kill your wife, and then I'm going to kill you!"

I know this voice was at least audible in my mind. Once again, an inaudible prayer of authority welled up from within me, and seconds later I was lying there trembling in a cold sweat. Anyone who tells you the forces of hell are not real is delusional and is trying to lead you down a path of ignorant disengagement. This was an all-out assault on my mind and my will to believe God.

In the midst of our trial, Diane and I were becoming more familiar with those demonic forces than we ever thought possible. We also became much more intimately acquainted with God's love for humanity. I tell this story only to illustrate that things were happening to us that sometimes made me think I was insane. I felt like one of the cast members of *One Flew Over the Cuckoo's Nest*. (For those of you who don't know, *One Flew Over the Cuckoo's Nest* is a brilliant movie from the 1970s, starring Jack Nicholson, that chronicled the lives of a small group of men who had experienced traumatic life events that caused their minds to go haywire, until they were permanently institutionalized.) The only reason I didn't have myself committed is because, as a seasoned spiritual leader, I'm familiar with the forces of darkness and how they work overtime to dismantle your mind and make you think you're crazy. Instances like these were all the more reason why Diane and I had to completely allow the mind of Christ to be in us and to surrender our wills in exchange for His.

An excerpt from the novel *This Present Darkness* describes how I was feeling.

> He stood in the dark and felt his courage deflated just
> that much more. He gripped the bat more tightly and
> moved down the hall, staying close to the wall,
> looking ahead, looking behind, listening. He thought

he could hear a quiet rustling somewhere, something moving. At the archway that led into the living room his eyes caught something, and he pressed himself against the wall for concealment. The front door was open. Now his heart really started pounding, thudding rudely in his ears. In a strange, jungle way he felt better; at least there was indication of a real enemy.[1]

ENDNOTE

1.   Frank Peretti, *This Present Darkness* (Carol Stream, IL: Living Books, 2002).

Chapter 12

"V" FOR VICTORY,
"W" FOR WILL

Nine requisites for contented living:
Health enough to make work a pleasure.
Wealth enough to support your needs.
Strength to battle with difficulties and overcome
   them.
Grace enough to confess your sins and forsake them.
Patience enough to toil until some good is
   accomplished.
Charity enough to see some good in your neighbor.
Love enough to move you to be useful and helpful to
   others.
Faith enough to make real the things of God.
Hope enough to remove all anxious fears concerning
   the future.
                                    —JOHANN VON GOETHE

The attitude of "going out" of which Oswald Chambers speaks is
exactly what Diane and I had to adopt. We had to wake each day
in a state of total surrender because we had no idea what the day was

going to bring. It's funny how most of us wake up each day with a quiet confidence that we already know how the day is going to turn out. We plan meetings, lunches, and outings and coordinate our whole day down to the minute. Sometimes it takes a critical situation to realize just how much we really do depend on God for every breath we take.

Since you really have no clue of the outcome of today, tomorrow, or any time in the future, now is the time to surrender your will in exchange for God's, so that you too can be confident that regardless of what comes your way, God is in control. This is especially true if you are right in the middle of a traumatic circumstance that's blindsided your life, similar to the way cancer intruded on our lives. One of the things that will become most evident to you in surrendering your will is how much more freedom you'll experience in the midst of trying times. This excerpt from a book by Jerry Sittser embellishes this point.

> The inability to predict the future was the first clue that set me searching in a different direction. But it was not the only clue I had. A second clue came from suffering loss. My wife Lynda and I had four wonderful children, two girls and two boys. We were deliriously happy. But that happiness—what we assumed was the "will of God" for our lives— came to a sudden halt in the fall of 1991 when a drunk driver jumped his lane and collided with our minivan, killing Lynda, my mother Grace, who was visiting for the weekend, and my daughter Diane Jane...That experience set me to thinking about the will of God. I had assumed that my marriage to Lynda was the will of God, that our family of six was the will of God, that the happy, stable, prosperous life we enjoyed together was the will of God ...I wondered how I could integrate suffering into my understanding of God's will. Or did God plan

something different for me, something still good,
but also hard and painful at the same time? If so, I
had to face the prospect that my approach to the
will of God was entirely mistaken.[1]

When Diane began her chemotherapy treatments, like most
patients, her hair began falling out in clumps. I distinctly remember
buying a pair of barber shears and standing in our bathroom, with
tears in my eyes, cutting Diane's hair. That simple act was part of the
surrender, an act of freedom and liberation. Diane refused to wear a
wig, although we did go to the mall one Saturday afternoon and
jokingly tried on a few. We had a great time that day!

A further demonstration of that surrender of wills came when it
was time for us to let the church know that Diane was suffering from
inoperable cancer. Just a few hours after I had sat in the bathroom
on Saturday night, watching the remaining clumps of Diane's hair
litter the floor, I was back on my post preparing to preach at our
Sunday morning service. At Mount Zion, before it's time for me to
preach we usually enjoy an extended period of praise and worship.
This particular Sunday morning was no different. I believe some
members had gotten word that Diane was ill, but they did not know
the full extent of her condition. I'm certain many were praising and
silently praying for her at the same time. Just as the worship portion
of the service was reaching its crescendo (at least what I thought was
going to be the apex of our experience that day), there was a rustling
in the back of the sanctuary. I looked up, and it was Diane walking
down the center aisle toward the front, her bald head reflecting the
hot lights. She was strolling toward the pulpit, praising God. With
worshipful confidence, her arms fully extended, she was holding up
two "V's" for Victory.

I probably don't have to tell you that what I thought was the
pinnacle of our praise had only been the bottom floor. Diane's
simple act of surrender to His will, and her liberation in front of our

entire congregation, took our worship to unimaginable heights. What was even more astonishing is that other cancer patients in the church began taking their wigs off and praising God in yielded humility to His will.

That memorable Sunday, Diane's act of walking down that aisle emotionally naked and not ashamed, preached a sermon far more impacting than any message I could have delivered. Diane only spoke briefly, but I distinctly remember her telling the congregation that her faith was strong, that she may have lost her hair, but that she wasn't going to lose her faith, and that she was completely dependent on God for everything. It truly was an authentic public surrender of a will that had already been relinquished in private.

An excerpt of the lyrics from a beautiful song by "India.Arie" authenticates what Diane demonstrated that day.

> *Because it was time to change my life*
> *To become the woman that I am inside*
> *Ninety-seven dreadlocks all gone*
> *I looked in the mirror*
> *For the first time and saw that, Hey…*

> *I am not my hair*
> *I am not this skin*
> *I am not your expectations, no, no*
> *I am not my hair*
> *I am not this skin*
> *I am a soul that lives within.*[2]

On that day, we all laughed together, cried together, and rejoiced together. Our emotions ran the gamut. If someone unfamiliar with our church had walked in on that scene, they probably would have thought that we all needed to be auditioning for the sequel to *One Flew Over the Cuckoo's Nest*. It's hard to completely describe the atmosphere. There were those who were sobbing with tears of grief, petitioning the Lord for a reprieve, and at the same time, others were laughing, shouting and doing a "victory" dance. I was experiencing and demonstrating a combination of both.

> *It's never a simple task to surrender your will in exchange for God's, especially when you learn that the two may be diametrically opposite to one another. But the beauty of doing so is that it's the first step to starting your soul on the road to complete healing and restoration, regardless of what's ahead.*

If I've learned nothing else about human emotions, I have discovered that each us responds to circumstances with a distinct emotional response. We each have our own innate way of allowing our emotions to help us process the sometimes harsh realities of life. Looking back, I can see that day was a training ground for the emotional roller coaster that lay ahead.

There's an amusement park in California called Knott's Berry Farm. One of the things Knott's Berry Farm is famous for is a roller coaster at the park called *Montezuma's Revenge*. The ride itself only lasts about 30 seconds, but people stand in line for hours to experience those 30 seconds. *Montezuma's Revenge* is known for the sheer torque, power, and speed that's unleashed once you've been strapped in. The coaster literally goes from 0–60 miles per hour in about 1.5 seconds. The burst of energy is almost overwhelming to the senses. I felt like Diane and I had been, unsuspectingly, trapped in a cycle of perpetual rides on *Montezuma's Revenge,* only we had been placed in the seats with the broken safety straps! Dietrich Bonhoeffer best describes how we were feeling.

> Have you ever, on a cold autumn night in the forest, heard the piercing cry of a deer? The whole forest shudders with the cry of longing. In the same way here, a human soul longs, not for some earthly good, but for God. Godly persons whose God has become remote from them, long for the God of salvation and grace. They know the God they long for; here are no seekers after an unknown God, who will never find anything. At some point they have experienced God's help and nearness. Thus they do not have to cry into a void. They call to their God…

> *"Succor me in fear and need Faithful God, have mercy on me! Your beloved child I remain, Despite Satan, world and every stain."*[3]

ENDNOTES

1.   Jerry Sittser, *The Will of God as a Way of Life* (Grand Rapids, MI: Zondervan, 2004).

2.   India.Arie, "I Am Not My Hair," *Testimony: Vol. 1, Life and Relationship* (Motown, 2006).

3.   Dietrich Bonhoeffer, *A Testament to Freedom: The Essential Writings of Dietrich Bonhoeffer* (New York: Harper, 1990).

Chapter 13

CRY ME A RIVER

When we believe that God is Father, we also believe
that such a father's hand will never cause his child
a needless tear. We may not understand life any
better, but we will not resent life any longer.
—WILLIAM BARCLAY

When dealing with emotions, it can often be difficult for
someone who is dealing with heartbreak and anguish to
express his or her emotions in a healthy manner. One of the most
refreshing lessons I learned during Diane's illness, and particularly
on the day of that glorious church service, is that it's OK to cry. To
my female readers, that statement almost sounds trite and simplistic.
Most women already have a pretty good understanding of this fact
and usually have no problem having a good cry to rinse the soul of
emotional debris. But sometimes it's even hard for women to cry.

Two of our most ardent supporters during this trial were Drs. Carl
and Andrea Willis. Diane affectionately referred to Carl as "Nerd Boy"
because the guy's like a walking encyclopedia. Not only is he a brilliant

doctor, but Carl also seemed to be able to regurgitate interesting facts about all sorts of stuff. His wisdom and wealth of medical knowledge was indeed a Godsend while we were battling with the unknown of inoperable cancer.

His wife, Andrea, is a brilliant doctor in her own right. She became known as the "Truth Bearer" because every time Diane had more tests done and the doctor would give us a diplomatic explanation of the results, Andrea would remove the sugarcoating and tell us the real deal.

I mention the Willis' here because after Diane died, Andrea shared a poignant story from an emotional moment she had with Diane that directly relates to the theme of this chapter—crying. Here's her verbatim account of the encounter.

> One day, we were visiting the Walker home. The men had gone in the other room, and I was alone with Diane. Tears welled up in her eyes. She was writhing with pain, shaking her foot, as if rocking herself. We both liked to think we were tough. We liked to bump fists rather than hug, but at this moment, I just wanted to ease her pain. As she was lying there, I got on my knees on the floor next to the bed, and I put my forehead against hers and wrapped my arms around her. I told her, "I'm not going soft, but I think you probably need this right now." She smiled. I asked her if she wanted me to let her go. She said, "No." I asked, "Why are you crying?" She paused for a minute, waiting for the nausea to pass, and then she said, "I'm mad at the pain." I told her I was mad too, and we continued to embrace.

Hearing that story made me tear up like never before. I didn't have a clue about the power of crying because historically I (and I think I can probably speak for most men) was not a crier. But during Diane's illness, I would find myself driving down Interstate 65 and suddenly hot tears would be gathering on the lower part of the steering wheel. I'd catch a glimpse of something that reminded me of Diane at the peak of health. Instantly I was swept into a vortex of memories, then the tears would come.

You need to know that it's OK to cry some-times, even if it means for extended periods of time. Grief has stages and comes in waves. I'm no psychologist, but I do know that one of those stages includes the shedding of tears as a means of releasing emotions that are try-ing to suffocate you.

While at first I felt a little less than manly, and I would at times look around to make sure others didn't see this grown man driving down the Interstate boo-hooing, I always felt so refreshed and relieved afterward. Now when I feel that emotion welling up in my throat, instead of forcing it back into the pit of my stomach, I let it rain. If you and Mr. Tears have always had a distant relationship, the next time he comes around, let it rain, then pour. Water is purifying. Never underestimate the restorative power of your tears to cleanse your soul and wash hope onto the shallow banks of desperation and grief. Displaying emotion is OK. It means you're human.

I had to come to grips with this reality during Diane's illness because while I was outwardly going about my normal routine, preaching and acting as pastor to thousands, inwardly I was a blubbering mess. I don't know if I've read anything that better describes the state of my emotions than this wonderful excerpt from a book by Dr. Larry Crabb.

> Life can be tough. It can be tough for sincere Christians who have walked faithfully with Christ for many years. It can be so tough that the best you can do is just hold on. Nights can be darker than you feared. Your soul can feel so alone, so filled with agony, so untouched by love, that the most honest thing you can do is cry. The only alternative is rage, a powerful, destructive rage that in a moment of expression can give you the comforting sense that someone is finally administering justice. That's what fuels our spirit of revenge. It's a testimony to how desperately we're committed to finding ourselves apart from God that the choice to abandon ourselves to Him is often most powerfully made when life has dragged us to the brink of blasphemy. Until we know how close we come to giving up on God ("Look what He allowed to happen in my life!"), we'll know little of what it means to give ourselves fully to God.[1]

That's a beautiful passage that describes the exact state of my emotions during Diane's illness. You can probably very quickly put together a list of situations in your own life that may be pushing you to the brink of blaspheming God. It's when you get to that place that our first two lessons of dealing with your mind and surrendering your will in exchange for His become all the more important. It's when you get to that point, and you're teetering on the brink of insanity, that really the only thing left to do is begin to look at life from a humorous viewpoint.

ENDNOTE

1. Dr. Larry Crabb, *Shattered Dreams* (Colorado Springs: Water-Brook, 2001).

Chapter 14

COMIC REVIEW

Humor is merely tragedy standing on its head with its pants torn.

—IRVIN S. COBB

There are times when life can seem like a river of misfortune that occasionally intersects with a narrow stream of good luck. I don't believe in luck. I do believe that when life's circumstances are thrust upon us, both the horrific and the heroic, laughter is one of the things that neutralizes a bad situation and shines a spotlight on the good. Diane did not choose terminal illness, but she did make a conscious choice to keep laughing—cancer or no cancer.

I can remember standing around Diane's hospital bed with a small group of friends and family, tubes protruding from several places on her body, and intimidating machines all around us. Diane would feed off of our conversation, turning our comments into witty jokes and comebacks like she was center stage at the Apollo. The room would fill with laughter. For those moments that cloud of despair, the one that hovers over most hospital rooms, would evaporate and we all felt like springtime. Laughter really is contagious, and I'm convinced that it passes on more than a three-dimensional display of our dental work. Laughter transfers hope and divine expectation.

Take a moment to laugh with someone. Pay close attention in the midst of that laughter, and you'll be able to sense that laughter is the equivalent of your spirit smiling and rejoicing, irrespective of what's going on in your mind, body, and circumstances.

Thinking back on that time in the hospital, and Diane's ability to laugh in the face of the pain, reminded me of how humor had always been one of Diane's wonderful personality traits, and others shared in the joy of her great sense of humor. Dr. Andrea Willis wrote a wonderful dedication to Diane after her death that I believe illustrates the power of humor to encourage ourselves and others during trying times:

> This past summer, Diane and I were at her house, and we were reminiscing about childhood as we watched the lightning bugs flying around. Bishop was to return late that evening, so we decided that we were going to catch some of those lightning bugs, and put them in a jar with a note to him saying, "We left the light on for you!" This memory is fond to me because Diane did let her light shine before men, so that they saw her good works and God was glorified. If you see my light shining, part of it is a reflection of the light she shined on me, and on countless others she touched. To my dear friend, Diane, thank you for leaving the light on for me.

When analyzing the soul in times of trial, it becomes quite evident that the potent combination of the mind, will, and emotions can lend credence to the analogy of the mind being a battlefield—the place where life's victories are either won abdicated. In laughter and in tears, I can move on with a limp, crippled but wiser.

For Diane and I it became clear early on that after we'd battled for our sanity, struggled to surrender our wills in exchange for God's, and allowed our emotions to work through the traumatic stages of grieving, that another battle was being waged just beyond the next mountain—a physical confrontation.

Spiritual Lifelines for Your Soul

1. Although life's battle is often waged in your mind, it's not your mind that you want to surrender. Instead of waving a white flag in your mind and giving up, you must take the offensive with your mind. Fill it with the biblical truths and positive reinforcements that will maintain your sanity in the midst of the battle.

2. Now your will is something that you do need to surrender. Do not surrender it in a nonchalant manner, as if to say, "whatever happens, happens," but surrender your will confidently. Exchange it for God's will, knowing that whatever happens, happens for a very specific reason.

3. It's normal to have emotions, and it's human to display them. The important thing to remember is that your emotions can actually be an asset to your life when you view them as one of the "release valves" God has built into your DNA. This release valve allows you to work through grief and disappointment to a place of healing and wholeness.

SECTION III

Tuesday
THE PHYSICAL

No matter how hard we try, words simply cannot express the horror, the shock, and the revulsion we all feel over what took place in this nation on Tuesday morning. September 11 will go down in our history as a day to remember.

—BILLY GRAHAM

Chapter 15

CHEMICAL WARFARE

My veins are filled, once a week, with a Neapolitan carpet cleaner distilled from the Adriatic, and I am bald as an egg. However, I still get around and am mean to cats.

—JOHN CHEEVER

Tuesday, September 11, 2001, is a date that will forever be entrenched in the minds and hearts of the American people and many nations around the world. On that day terrorists hijacked planes going about their normal routines and transformed them into "sky bombs" used to destroy buildings and lives. Similarly, cancer overtakes the normal routine of your life, hijacks your body, and turns it into a ticking time bomb, set to explode at any time, bringing with it death and destruction.

Having watched Diane deal with the side effects of cancer and chemotherapy for months, I knew firsthand that the disease was more abominable than any terrorist could ever hope to be. I now understood why the ingredients for chemotherapy were also used as

101

chemical warfare agents. Deadly stuff! Like a bomb whose detonator had been set, there was no turning back the clock on what the cancer was doing to Diane's body. When Diane first became ill, both of us were mystified by what was happening to her body. Here's a journal entry I penned after the fact, which provides a glimpse into my head-space at the time.

Acid and Ulcers

A few months prior to that fateful day at the doctor's office, Diane had gone to see her primary care physician because she was experiencing stomach pains. It was nothing major. We both just thought she had a case of acid reflux or severe indigestion, not inoperable stomach cancer.

At the time, Mount Zion was experiencing explosive growth and we were transitioning into a new, multimillion-dollar church facility, so we took into consideration that stress could be causing some of Diane's stomach issues. It doesn't take much more than increased stress levels to trigger a painful ulcer. We had no idea we'd be waging a battle against something much more heinous than acid and ulcers.

Weeks and weeks of painful testing and multiple doctor visits revealed some much bigger demons. I purposely use the word "demons" because although Diane's diagnosis was very much a genuine physical condition, it was our conviction that anything that manifests in the natural first began in the spiritual.

Months later, I had a gruesome encounter that authenticated the dastardliness of the spiritual battle and provided a better understanding of the forces of both evil and good. But on the day that we learned it was something bigger than acid and ulcers, it felt like I had cancer too, or at least some of its side effects.

My body literally went into a state of shock after Diane was diagnosed. Not only did I begin to feel aches and pains all over, but I could not sleep. The fatigue and exhaustion were almost overwhelming.

While I had a sense in my spirit that things were worsening, my suspicions were confirmed when the doctor called. It was a hot summer day, but there was no sunshine in his voice. After the Monday I'd just experienced, I really wanted to just skip Tuesday altogether. This second journal entry recounts the day more vividly.

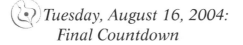 *Tuesday, August 16, 2004:*
Final Countdown

I remember this day so well because it remains an active part of my mental space. I was on my way to minister, sitting on a bus with the praise team, headed to a church out of town. Diane was home at the time. She was actually having a good day. Just a week prior, the doctor told us that the scan results were not good. The cancer was progressively taking over her liver.

I remember Diane's humor that day at the doctor's office, the week before I got the call. Here I was with tears in my eyes and the doctor with tears in his eyes, and Diane looking at us both calling us punks. She continued to tell the doctor she was going to be his miracle patient. I could tell that Diane's faith had started to give the doctor hope for the miraculous, even as he stared at the cold, hard reality of black masses on the x-rays. Even our good friend Dr. Andrea Willis, a woman full of faith, later shared with me that she wanted so bad to share in Diane's faithful optimism, but the medical side of her kept rearing it's ugly head shouting, "Andrea, this doesn't look good. We're in the fourth quarter and down to the two-minute warning."

When we left the office that day, Diane wanted me to go and purchase the new truck she'd been wanting for a long time. We went directly to the dealership and got that truck. She believed she was going to be around and wanted to live with that kind of conviction in mind. Less than a week after we drove off the lot in our brand new truck, full of hope and optimism, I was on that bus ride to minister when my cell phone rang.

It was Dr. Patton. He is such a nice man. Dr. Patton is undoubtedly a man of faith and compassion, yet on this call, his voice had more of a serious, objective tone. He told me that I needed to begin thinking about Diane's care because, based on the last scan, it was his assessment that she had six months to live.

I could feel my heart rapidly accelerate, as scorching tears began to run down my face. I wonder now in hindsight if Job had a similar emotional response when he got his bad news. Truthfully, by the time Dr. Patton called, I was so fatigued that I don't think I had the capacity for any more emotion than the quiet tears I shed on the bus that day. Part of that fatigue came from the routine Diane and I had started months before. It was a routine designed specifically to keep our faith alive. We would pray and I would read Psalm 119. It's a long Psalm, but she wanted to hear it almost every day. Consequently, we made time for this daily ritual in spite of my hectic schedule, and her physical struggles. We had a clipboard in our bedroom where we would post confessions of faith. There were sticky-notes all around the house with Scriptures and biblical promises on them. I had operated on little or no sleep many nights, interceding for Diane and comforting her. Yet, in that moment I felt like I had begun a new race.

When you come to moments like that you have to realize that His strength is made perfect in your weakness. I knew the enemy was attempting to beat us down until the fight left us, but we knew we had to intensify our efforts. I waited until I got home that evening to tell Diane.

When I told her, she smiled again and declared, "That's what they say, but I know what God says." No matter how negative the report, you have to have the resolve to believe God for a miracle. Diane did not waiver in her faith. She stood strong and again asked me to read Psalm 119. It was at that moment I noticed a shift in Diane. She would spend hours in her office with the door closed. I honestly believed that she moved to a place in her spirit where she needed to work through some things with God for herself. This was not a bad thing. Each of us must "steal away" to our own private world and work through our issues with God's will, so that we can be in a better position to fight when we are confronted.

When I received that news, it was as if someone had turned an hourglass upside down. I knew we were racing against the clock. Those tumors were growing. My faith had to go to another level. She needed me and I needed God. Job says in Job 14:14, "All of my appointed time will I wait till my change comes." We had been given an appointed time of 6 months, and all we could do is believe God for a change to come. When you are fighting time, you watch every minute and every second. Things you used to take for granted no longer are overlooked. Every moment I had with Diane was more precious than any had been before.

When you're going through a rough season in your life, it's important that you find routine things to do, no matter how simple, that can keep that small flame of faith burning. For Diane and I, it was Psalm 119. For you, it might be a different Scripture or a daily walk. Whatever it is, find it and maintain it.

Needless to say, with a six-month sentence Diane and I began to reprioritize. Reading the words of a college professor (who had also been diagnosed with pancreatic cancer) reminded me of how I felt about life when Dr. Patton gave me the news.

That very week, however, I got the news: My most recent treatment hadn't worked. I had just months to live. I knew I could cancel the lecture. Everyone would understand. Suddenly, there were so many other things to be done. I had to deal with my own grief and the sadness of those who loved me. I had to throw myself into getting my family's affairs in order. And yet, despite everything, I couldn't shake the idea of giving the talk. I was energized by the idea of delivering a last lecture that really was a last lecture.[1]

Similar to the way Randy Pausch pondered the content of his "last lecture," I began to really contemplate how Diane and I would spend our remaining time together. I also became intensely focused on Diane's physical health, and the lessons I'd learned about our bodies throughout the illness. If you read further in Randy Pausch's book, one of the main things he was concerned about with respect to giving his lecture, and even writing the book, was whether or not his body was going to hold out long enough for him to see the projects through to completion. (It did—he passed away in July 2008, one month after his book became a bestseller).

As I thought about the frailty of our human bodies, three things came to mind: (1) the heavy toll stressful circumstances were having on our bodies, (2) the need to learn how we could find victory in the midst of physical challenges, and (3) the need to learn how we could begin rebuilding our bodies in preparation for a lifetime of healthy service to others. These thoughts continued to guide my thinking as I considered the importance of the physical realm.

ENDNOTE

1. Randy Pausch, *The Last Lecture* (New York: Hyperion, 2008).

Chapter 16

DON'T STRESS AROUND

I try to take one day at a time, but sometimes several days attack me at once.

—JENNIFER YANE

While cancer was ravaging Diane's body, the stress of what it was doing to her, coupled with all of my responsibilities, was destroying mine. I know the entire theme of this book has been about giving difficulties to God and persevering through tough times, but I would be a hypocrite if I didn't honestly admit that, at times, I was stressed out of my gourd. Some days I didn't eat at all. Other days, I ate enough for three or four people. I'm certain my body thought that I was playing some sort of cruel game. Reading through *Stress Management for Dummies* provided a very real wake-up call.

> Stress can play a role in circulatory diseases such as coronary heart disease, sudden cardiac death and strokes. This fact is not surprising because stress can

increase your blood pressure, constrict your blood vessels, raise your cholesterol level, trigger arrhythmias, and speed up the rate at which your blood clots. Stress is now considered a major risk factor in heart disease, right up there with smoking, being overweight, and a lack of exercise. All of this becomes very important when you consider that heart disease kills more men over the age of 50 and more women over the age of 65 than any other disease.[1]

Control your stress levels with a big daily dose of God's Word. He has the answer for every problem.

Reading that one small excerpt forced me to realize that not only did I have to build my spirit and protect my soul, but it was also imperative that I guard my body from stress. At that point in my journey with Diane's illness, I was already suffering from severe physical exhaustion and fatigue. Stress was the third—and most devastating—threat in the "triple threat" assault on my body. It was as if Diane and I were both having physical breakdowns simultaneously. A journal entry reminded me of her crippling physical challenges.

Scared to Life

I thought Diane died tonight. I titled this journal entry "Scared to Life" because she didn't. Like every other Sunday, I preached my heart all day, and returned this evening exhausted in spirit, mind, and body. I've been thinking about Diane all day and couldn't wait to get home to see her. Every time I preach now, I feel a sting of pain. I think it's caused by two things: I feel guilty that I'm at the church preaching and not home with her, and my heart breaks when I am preaching and I glance down to that empty seat where Diane used to sit, my number one cheerleader. That hurts. Having thought about Diane all day, and battling the conflicting inner struggle of doing what God's called me to do, and longing to hold my wife, as soon as the altar call was over, I sped home and rushed in to see Diane. Finding her lying there motionless on the floor was horrifying. In the back of my mind, I'd been trying to mentally prepare myself for dealing with the unfortunate possibility of discovering Diane's lifeless body. I still have some work to do because I wasn't prepared tonight. In fact, I probably won't ever be ready for that moment. When I spotted Diane, I could feel the panic starting to overtake my body. The only thing I knew to do was run down the street and grab Dr. Rogers, who lives four houses away. He immediately came back with me and found that Diane was extremely dehydrated and had passed out as a result. To say I was relieved would be like O.J. saying he felt a sense of relief when that "not guilty" verdict was read. I felt a sense of God saying, "Not today."

That day my stress levels were off the charts, and Diane's body was failing. I knew that we both had to somehow discover some hidden paths to victory in the midst of such overwhelming physical challenges.

You too may be facing enormous physical constraints that are causing a degree of stress that's difficult for your body to process. There are ways to experience hopeful milestones in spite of extreme physical limitations, as I discovered.

ENDNOTE

1.   Allen Elkin, *Stress Management for Dummies* (Foster City, CA: IDG Books, 1999).

Chapter 17

VICTORY IN THE HOME STRETCH

The execution of any thing considerable implies in the first place previous persevering meditation.

—WILLIAM GODWIN

I honestly believe that Randy Pausch, the author of *The Last Lecture,* extended his life by determining that he needed more time in order to find victory for himself and others, not in spite of his physical challenges but because of them.

When the body begins to break down, it can be a horrible thing. This excerpt from an international bestseller reminded me of the brutal realities of physical demise.

> At eight-thirty, the physical therapist arrives. Brigitte, a woman with an athletic figure and an imperial Roman profile, has come to exercise my stiffened arms and legs. They call the exercise "mobilization," a term whose martial connotations contrast ludicrously with

113

the paltry forces thus summoned, for I've lost sixty-six pounds in just twenty weeks. When I began a diet a week before my stroke, I never dreamed of such a dramatic result. As she works, Brigitte checks for the smallest flicker of improvement. "Try to squeeze my hand," she asks. Since I sometimes have the illusion that I am moving my fingers, I focus my energy on crushing her knuckles, but nothing stirs and she replaces my inert hand on its foam....[1]

Although Diane had experienced physical challenges for years, good health was extremely important to her, as was helping others to better their own health. Always a doer, even while battling cancer, Diane teamed up with her good friend Dr. Andrea Willis to host an event at the church called "Search Your Heart." The primary goal of "Search Your Heart" was to empower people in the city of Nashville with the tools and resources to get educated about the importance of a healthy body, mind, and spirit. The event was a tremendous success and a service to the whole community. Diane truly understood the principle of gaining victory over your own physical challenges by helping others gain victory over theirs.

Gain victory over your physical challenges by helping others gain victory over theirs. Reach out to someone who is hurting.

I even walked away from the event with some very helpful concepts for dealing with Diane's private physical struggle, as well as my own battle with stress and tangible fatigue. The main thing I learned was that if I wanted to continue to be an effective leader I was going to have to make some drastic adjustments with respect to my health.

If you are in a difficult trial that does not end quickly, taking care of your physical well-being is not something that can just wait until the crisis is over. You need to care for your body even while your mind, will, and emotions are still fighting the battle.

ENDNOTE

1.   Jean-Dominique Bauby, *The Divine Bell and the Butterfly: A Memoir of Life in Death* (New York: Random House, 1997).

PREPARATION FOR SERVICE

Health is not valued till sickness comes.
—THOMAS FULLER

One of the most important things you can do is monitor your physical health with a program that includes proper diet, vigorous exercise, and regular visits to the doctor. Believe me when I tell you that you don't want to be caught in the position of finding out that something is wrong with you when it's too late to medically treat it. I felt like that was the dilemma Diane and I were facing, which was reinforced by some of the frustrating medical problems Diane had been experiencing for several years.

I'm not saying that poor habits and an unhealthy lifestyle caused Diane to come down with pancreatic cancer. To the contrary, Diane was always quite active, and being a student by nature, she was very consistent with exercise and eating nutritiously. I am saying that for many of you, getting things in order with your health could very well be an offensive, preventative measure against future bouts with terminal illness. More importantly, a combination of proper diet and

117

exercise will help you to be 100 percent effective in every area of your life.

A passage from a great book on godly nutrition was my first wake-up call.

> You are important and have a mission and purpose in life which only you can fulfill. You are responsible for your own health status. It matters not whether you are a doctor, a pastor, a lawyer, a maintenance engineer, a common laborer or a housewife. Regardless of your occupation, your health depends on whether you are obedient to natural law or whether you violate it. If you violate natural law by insisting on putting toxic foods in your body, how can you expect to be well? What performance would you expect from your car if you insisted on filling it with cheap, low-grade, junk fuel, contrary to the recommendations of its manufacturer? The same principle applies to our bodies.... I urge you to learn God's natural laws for health and apply them in your life so these natural laws can benefit you with the blessings of health, high spirits and longevity rather than allowing these natural laws to make you downcast with sickness, disabilities and a premature death.[1]

Although that passage may seem a little heavy-handed, with the way that Diane's body was literally failing, a little heavy-handedness seemed like a small price to pay for learning what I needed to do to take care of my body and to help Diane to live as comfortably as possible in hers.

I almost hate to admit it, but while the church is supposed to be a place to help people live victorious lives, it can be notorious for practicing and promoting extremely unhealthy eating habits. I've been to far too many church functions where the food smelled like ten extra pounds, deep-fried in high blood pressure, marinated with some extra cholesterol, and then served over a generous helping of diabetes.

When Diane became ill, the right diet became acutely important. She was taking so many medications, and her body reacted so negatively to them, that anything but the most wholesome and natural foods spelled big trouble. From Diane's experience, I began to realize that her body was rejecting what's commonly referred to as "junk food" because of her debilitated state. But really, all of our bodies reject that type of food, we just don't experience the extreme negative side effects while our immune systems are strong.

Getting things in order with your health could very well be an offensive, preventative measure against future bouts with terminal illness.

But once those defenses are broken down, "junk food" ravages your body. If you've ever been sick during Thanksgiving or Christmas dinner, you know exactly what I'm talking about. While everyone else is gorging themselves on ham, turkey, stuffing, and pumpkin pie, all you can manage is some fruit and a glass of water. That's your body telling you, "I'd really prefer that you eat this light all of the time, but right now I'm forcing you to do so because I'm pretty much defenseless right now against that heavy meal you're eyeing."

That's how Diane's body was responding 24/7 when she became ill, and it forced me to realize that I needed to make some dietary adjustments as well. Although our dietary adjustments were based on urgent necessity—and yours may be too—I want to recommend that you start moving in the right direction today by educating yourself about the foods you need to be eating and making a conscious decision to change your dietary practices. While a better body and an extended healthy life may be two of your reasons for taking action, the primary focus should be on doing so in order to be 100 percent effective in serving others and completing your life's purpose.

An amazing book for getting your body together in preparation for fulfilling a greater purpose is *Body for Life* by Bill Phillips. Here's an excerpt to encourage you to get started today.

> It was at this point Lynn began searching for answers. He started having vivid dreams of being a competitive athlete, of being strong and hopeful, with life stretching out in front of him like a bright sunlit path, rather than the dark, hollow tunnel he had been seeing. He hauled himself to a local gym and began asking around for information on how to get in shape. One of the guys in the room handed him a copy of one of my publications. Lynn recounts, "I had never been so fat. I didn't know what type of nutrition or exercise program I should be following. I looked at this magazine and really liked the way it was written …Beyond information, I was being taught a frame of mind, which inspired me more than all the preachers, teachers, doctors, and counselors who had tried to get through to me before. I couldn't fight the HIV virus physically. I mean, you can't punch it and beat it up. But every time I finished a hard workout, I felt like I

had won a battle. Every day I stuck with my nutrition program, I felt like I had taken one more step to climb out of the hole I had dug for myself.[2]

Diane and I felt like we were in a deep pit when we learned of her illness. Beyond reinforcing our spirits and souls with prayer and Bible study, it was the combination of proper nutrition and exercise that helped add some glimmer of hope to a dire situation. That combination is what helped Diane continue to lead somewhat of a normal lifestyle until just a couple of months before she died. It's also partly what allowed me to continue preaching and carrying out my pastoral duties during her illness.

I learned this lesson during a dark time. But if you work on the physical area of your life now, it can really help you to stay strong for whatever you may face in the future.

ENDNOTES

1.   Dr. George Malkmus, *God's Way to Ultimate Health* (Shelby, NC: Hallelujah Acres Publishing, 1995).

2.   Bill Phillips, *Body for Life* (New York: HarperCollins, 1999).

Chapter 19

EXERCISE—THE GREAT ELIXIR

> All parts of the body which have a function if used in
> moderation and exercised in labors in which each is
> accustomed, become thereby healthy, well developed
> and age more slowly, but if unused they become
> liable to disease, defective in growth and age quickly.
> — HIPPOCRATES

Throughout the decades, all sorts of diet books have claimed to
have found the latest, greatest cures for obesity and poor
health. We've had the Beverly Hills Diet, the Atkins Diet, the
Maker's Diet, and the list goes on and on. With thousands of books,
all with different titles but saying pretty much the same thing, it's
interesting that having a healthy body really just boils down to
eating sensibly and moderately exercising a few times a week. We
make everything so complicated. With Diane's cancer, further
complications to our lives were the last thing we were looking for.
We wanted simplicity in all forms. Exercise became just being able
to take a walk together and talk.

I wonder how many couples out there could overhaul their marriages and their bodies if they just took an hour a day to walk and talk. Diane and I had some of our most intimate conversations when we just walked and talked. It didn't matter if we were in the park or in the mall; we were exercising our bodies and knitting our hearts together. That's my simple advice for the physical portion of this book: just walk and talk. If you have a companion, walk and talk with them. If not, find a place of solitude and pray while walking.

I'll forever cherish those times I had walking with Diane. In the end, we couldn't walk very far because she'd get what she referred to as episodes (vomiting and diarrhea) that would cut things short. Sometimes we'd be right in the middle of a walk, and she'd say, "Oh &%#@, I feel an episode coming on!" That would mean it was time to get back to the house or to the nearest restroom in a hurry. I share this story without embarrassment because I want it to encourage you to appreciate the health that you do have and to take the necessary steps now to improve it. And if you are presently in poor health, it's my hope that my transparency will inspire you to persevere in the midst of the illness the way Diane did.

Sadly, there did come a time when Diane was no longer able to walk. The last service she attended at our church was in December 2004. By that time, Diane's favorite seat was removed from its spot in the front of the sanctuary and replaced by the wheelchair she then needed to get around. I knew then that twilight was settling on Tuesday, and this particular Wednesday was going to be a very difficult "hump day."

Spiritual Lifelines for Your Body

1. Recognize that stress can be a silent but powerful enemy, especially in times of great crisis. There's no better stress reducer than prayer and meditation on God's Word. In tough times, take offen-

sive action against stress by combating it with biblical truth.

2. A basic program of proper nutrition and exercise could be the "miracle" that you're looking for. Be proactive now to start a program and allow it to be your "miracle." This could prevent you from getting to the place where you really do require divine intervention.

3. Instead of getting overwhelmed by complicated books and programs, start by consulting your physician and starting a basic program that includes a sensible diet and walking a few times a week.

SECTION IV

Wednesday
THE EDUCATIONAL

We'll see where he's at come Wednesday and we'll
determine what we're going to do.

—HERMAN EDWARDS

Chapter 20

MEDICAL SCHOOL REMIX

To learn is to change. Education is a process that changes the learner.

—AUTHOR UNKNOWN

Like the aforementioned quote, I had to wait until Wednesday to see where Diane was "at" and what we were going to do. Wednesday is often referred to as "hump day" because you've been able to climb up to the middle of the week, to the center of the "hump," and now you're at a point where you can coast down the other side through the rest of the week, or trip and tumble down to Saturday. Either way, there's no going back. You're going over the "hump" either walking or rolling.

For us, Wednesday definitely represented the point in Diane's illness where all of our strength had been sapped, and we were either going to have to be carried through the rest of the week or we'd just roll down without a care of whether or not we made it to the bottom alive. After we'd determined to build our spirits, minds, and bodies, one of the few other things that brought some comfort was educating ourselves about the enemy that we were fighting (cancer). Based on our backgrounds and curious minds, I knew getting a thorough knowledge and understanding of cancer was not going to be a problem.

From the time I was a young child, I had a voracious appetite for education. I would read books while other kids played. I was always curious and intrigued by the world. Diane was the same way from her youth and all the way through dentistry school. Neither of us knew exactly how much we would come to appreciate our inquisitive personalities until after her diagnosis. Any sports coach will tell you that knowing your opponent can make games much easier, even when your opponent outmatches you on paper. That's why coaches and athletes spend hours and hours studying film of their opponents, looking for weaknesses and ways to gain an advantage.

That's how Diane and I approached the cancer. We knew that educating ourselves about what we were fighting would not only serve as therapy, but would also show us where and how we needed to apply our faith. It was almost as if we went back to medical school. We got on the Internet. We read books. And we had friends who served as some of the best personal "professors" in the world. Dr. Karl Rogers, the cancer director at Baptist Hospital, was a neighbor, and Drs. Carl and Andrea Willis were a constant source of friendship and medical information in our lives.

Educating ourselves about Diane's cancer didn't eradicate the realities of dealing with the disease. But it did provide us with the opportunity to learn about a disease that was—at the same time it was ravaging Diane's body—also decimating the lives of millions of others around the world. It was therapeutic to know that this wasn't our singular, lonely struggle. God hadn't singled us out to deal with a disease that no one had ever battled or heard of. So while we prayed for Diane, we also prayed for the millions of others who were waging similar battles. Here's a brief, moving passage that reveals another's struggle with what we were facing.

Outside, the sun was shining and people were going

130

about their business. A woman ran to put money in the parking meter. Another carried groceries. Charlotte had a million thoughts running through her mind: *How much time do we have left? How will we manage? How will we pay the bills?* My old professor, meanwhile, was stunned by the normalcy of the day around him. *Shouldn't the world stop? Don't they know what has happened to me?* But the world did not stop, it took no notice at all, and as Morrie pulled weakly on the car door, he felt as if he were dropping into a hole. *Now what?* he thought.[1]

Our struggle was not an isolated incident of cruel judgment. That was very important for us because when terminal illness or a tragic incident invades your life, you feel like you've been singled out. Diane and I became educated to the fact that others were fighting, praying, and persevering just like we were. Educating ourselves about cancer from that perspective was very therapeutic. It was therapeutic in the sense that we had the knowledge for ourselves, but also because it allowed us to share with others who were frightened by the mystery of an incurable disease. We found that unraveling that mystery actually brought healing to others and eased their fears as well.

If I'm going to die, I'd much rather know how I'm dying and have a clear understanding of the progression of it all, rather than wait for it to mysteriously happen one day. I'm not saying it makes dealing with terminal illness easy, but it does make it more palatable. It's like a woman giving birth to a baby. The expectant mother reads all sorts of books about what she will experience before, during, and after the birth. She educates herself about the step-by-step process of actually giving birth. The books describe the potent waves of pain, the feelings of anxiety, and the intense desire for it all to be over. On the day she gives birth, the expectant mother does in fact experience all the things she'd read about. The pain isn't any less real because she read about it, but she is able to better endure it since she knew it was coming.

When Diane's health took a severe turn for the worse, we knew it was coming, and we knew why. Not only had recent tests revealed that the cancer was spreading and the tumors were growing, but we had read about how the cancer goes about doing what it does best: destroying the body. And destruction is exactly what it brought to Diane's body. Diane and I were doing what's called "offensive study," a technique described best by the great author Gordon MacDonald.

> In my earliest years of ministry, when this business of mental growth had not yet become a discipline for me, most of my study was what I now call *defensive study*. By that I mean that I studied frantically simply because I had an upcoming sermon to preach or talk to give. And all my study was centered on the completion of that task.
>
> But later I discovered the importance of something I now call *offensive study*. This is study that has as its objective the gathering of large clusters of information and insight out of which future sermons and talks, books, and articles may grow. In the former kind of study, one is restricted to one chosen subject. In the latter, one is exploring, turning up truth and understanding from scores of sources....
>
> We grow when we pursue the discipline of offensive study.[2]

I started gathering information in large "clusters" because I knew it was going to be useful for future sermons, discussions, and counseling sessions. I also wanted to find a way to inspire others to pursue education.

Diane's passion for education is one of the reasons why I started the

Diane Greer-Walker Memorial Scholarship Fund after her death. I wanted to give others the opportunity to combat spiritual, social, physical, and financial challenges through education. A spiritual education means you'll have an understanding of biblical truths and how to apply them to your life. A social understanding means you'll have a realization that we live in a diverse world that requires tolerance, love, and compassion for the betterment of all humankind. A physical education means you'll truly comprehend the importance of taking care of your body to ensure long-term health and the ability to serve others with 100-percent effectiveness. A financial education means you will grasp the significance of financial stewardship as a means of eliminating indebtedness and creating generational wealth.

While I was already very big on education and providing others with the tools to better their knowledge, Diane's cancer definitely took this up a notch. Whatever difficulties you're facing right now, think of ways in which educating yourself about the anatomy of those problems may bring about solutions that will become a benefit to your own life, as well as those in your sphere of influence.

The Diane Greer-Walker Memorial Scholarship Fund has turned into an annual Celebrity Basketball Game where hundreds of families come together to share in food, fun, and a sense of community. We're providing the community with an opportunity to fellowship, but more importantly, we're giving away tangible scholarships to kids who realize the weightiness of obtaining a proper education.

And this was all birthed out of walking into a doctor's office one day and getting some of the worst news one could possibly receive. It's just further proof that all things really do work together for the good of those who love God and are called according to His purpose.

It was that very purpose that Diane and I were going to have to cling to as Wednesday came to a close. And by educating ourselves we had become fully aware of exactly what we were facing. It wasn't a pretty picture, but we knew that in spite of the trial God was still fulfilling His purpose in our lives, and that's what kept us going.

Meanwhile, the moment we get tired of waiting, God's Spirit is right alongside helping us along. If we don't know how or what to pray, it doesn't matter. He does our praying in and for us, making prayer out of our wordless sighs, our aching groans. He knows us far better than we know ourselves, knows our pregnant condition, and keeps us present before God. That's why we can be so sure that every detail in our lives of love for God is worked into something good (Romans 8:28 The Message).

Spiritual Lifelines for Your Education

1. In difficult times, use education as a tool to understand your problems. While understanding them may not make them go away, it will provide you with an offensive weapon to persevere in the midst of them.

2. People in other countries are ravenous for education. The United States has one of the most extensive library systems in the world, yet our libraries are like ghost towns, and our kids are dropping out of school at alarming rates. Value your freedom and opportunities, which are the fruit of a good education.

3. While education serves as therapy for your own troubles, let it also serve as a tool for service to others in the form of spiritual, social, and economic empowerment.

ENDNOTES

1. Mitch Albom, *Tuesdays With Morrie* (New York: Doubleday, 1997).

2. Gordon MacDonald, *Ordering Your Private World* (Nashville: Thomas Nelson, 1985), 109.

SECTION V

Thursday
THE VOCATIONAL

I didn't think the subject matter of Thursday's show was the kind of broadcast that I should be doing. I suggested some alternatives, but the producers preferred the topics they had chosen.

—BOB COSTAS

Chapter 21

THE GREAT PRODUCER

To be glad of life, because it gives you the chance to love and to work and to play and to look up at the stars; to be satisfied with your possessions, but not contented with yourself until you have made the best of them; to despise nothing in the world except falsehood and meanness, and to fear nothing except cowardice; to be governed by your admirations rather than by your disgusts; to covet nothing that is your neighbor's except is kindness of heart and gentleness of manners; to think seldom of your enemies, and often of your friends, and very day of Christ; and to spend as much time as you can, with body and with spirit, in God's out-of-doors—these are little guideposts on the footpath to peace.

—HENRY VAN DYKE

In the making of a feature film, the producer is responsible for overseeing the managerial and financial aspects of the movie. The role is such an important one that if a film doesn't have a producer, it usually doesn't get made. One thing we know for sure is that God is the ultimate "Producer," orchestrating the affairs of our lives with expert precision. And while we don't always agree with the subject matter, we must still trust Him as the great "Producer" and "Director" of human affairs. There's no arguing with the storyline of our lives that He's already scripted.

While growing up in Shreveport, Louisiana, I had my heart set on being a lawyer. My older brother Michael was a lawyer, and I wanted to follow in his footsteps. Even while working toward my undergraduate degree at Southern University, I just knew law school would be my next stop. At the time, I never even considered being a preacher. The only time the name Joseph Walker and "preacher" were ever mentioned in the same sentence was when my grandmother wanted to reminisce. She reminded me when I was as a young boy (aged 7 or 8), we attended a special church service where some ministers were being honored. According to my grandmother, I told her that I wanted to go stand with the preachers being recognized and she allowed me to. As long as she was alive, she often told me that God showed her on that day that I was going to be a preacher.

During my teenage years, I just chuckled politely when she shared the story, while in my mind's eye I was on my way to being the next Johnnie Cochran. It's funny how God will only let us continue on a path for so long before he intersects our lives with destiny, and we're never the same going forward. After graduating from Southern with a B.A. in English, instead of staying at Southern to attend law school, I ended up hundreds of miles east, studying for a Masters in Divinity at Vanderbilt University in Nashville, Tennessee. Had I not listened to the counsel of my pastor at the time, I might have gone down the wrong fork in the road.

Over the years, I had built a tremendous confidence that I would become an outstanding lawyer, but preaching? I felt so unprepared for divinity school. This was a time that I really did have to learn that God's strength is made perfect in my weakness, and maybe He actually could work with the little faith I had that preaching might in fact be my life's calling.

Chapter 22

WORK WITH WHAT YOU'VE GOT

Opportunity is missed by most people because it is dressed in overalls and looks like work.

—THOMAS EDISON

I think we have all missed out on opportunities in our lives because we've felt that somehow we wouldn't quite fit in or the decision didn't quite jibe with how we had already planned things out. I know there have been times in my own life when great occasions for new friendships, rekindled relationships, or just fresh adventures have slipped through into yesterday. Whether it was my skin color, my bank account, or just a general feeling of inadequacy, I know at one time or another one or more of these reasons have been the culprit of missed opportunities.

How many class reunions have been purposely skipped, the chance to see old friends gone forever, because some of the invitees felt the sum total of their life's work didn't quite add up enough to merit their atten-dance? What I admired about Diane was her willingness to take full advantage of every opportunity irrespective of her personal circumstances. It's a lesson I think she learned from her humble beginnings in Winona, Mississippi.

I'm sure you've probably heard it before, but God really is not looking for superstars. Throughout the Bible, He demonstrates time and again that His ultimate purpose is best fulfilled in ordinary, yielded people. And often, it was in the midst of a crisis that those ordinary people were used the most.

Don't allow life to pass you by because you feel as if you don't quite fit. There's healing in knowing you're fine just the way you are. If I had allowed feelings of inadequacy to control my actions at that critical turning point when my pastor assisted with my admission to Vanderbilt, I might have never ended up in Nashville, or met Diane. You may have some crucial decisions that you need to make in your own life right now. Don't make those decisions based on your inadequacies. Make those decisions based on the knowledge that the strength to do the right thing will come from God as you step out in faith and obedience.

Chapter 23

SUPERSTARS NEED NOT APPLY

Excellence is doing ordinary things extraordinarily well.
—JOHN W. GARDNER

As mentioned previously, the thing that I learned very early in ministry is that God is not looking for superstars. Being a person with a Type "A" (ambitious, driven, impatient) personality, I often had a tendency to jump ahead of God and "make" things happen in the name of doing His will and fulfilling His purpose for my life. I've never seen anything more effective than an unassailable trial to bring "superstar ambitions" to a screeching halt. That's the kind of "smoking brakes" STOP that Diane and I came to when we discovered she had cancer.

At the time, we were "superstar servants." We had one church with two locations and a third being constructed. I was hopping all over the globe preaching. Diane was teaching, working in the medical field, and leading the women's ministry at the church. And then cancer said, "STOP!"

As I look back on it now, I can see clearly that God didn't cause the cancer, but He did allow it to be used as a tool to help further refine

143

and define our purposes, both individually and collectively. We already had an understanding that God had a purpose for our lives, but now the vision was getting ready to become crystal clear. The fact that we couldn't just quit what we were doing because Diane had cancer was the most significant indication that God's purpose was being fulfilled through our vocation and the vision was real. A passage from a great book by Andy Stanley describes it well.

> Vision translates into purpose. A vision gives you a reason to get up in the morning. If you don't show up, something important won't be accomplished. Suddenly, you matter. You matter a lot! Without you, what could be—what should be—won't be. A vision makes you an important link between current reality and the future. That dynamic gives your life purpose. And purpose carries with it the momentum to move you through the barriers that would otherwise slow you down and trip you up. Your set of visions are unique to you. No one else will share your particular passions for what could be. Others may applaud them. They may buy into aspects of your vision that interface with their life. And they may work with you in the areas where you share a common vision. But your vision-set is unique to you. This uniqueness gives your life purpose. You have a reason for getting up and showing up.[1]

With Diane's cancer, we definitely had a barrier that was trying to trip us up, but the purpose and vision inside of us wouldn't let us stop. One of the most simplistic and beautiful verses in the Bible is found in the Book of Jeremiah, where God says to Jeremiah, "Before I formed you in the womb I knew you, before you were born I set you apart..." (Jer. 1:5). I love that passage because it means that we were all formed to fulfill a specific purpose in the earth.

Regardless of what your vocation is right now, you were created by God to fulfill a purpose in the earth. In fact, your vocation can be one of the tools that God uses to fulfill His purpose.

When Diane became extremely ill, her vocation became "survivor." As a "survivor" she inspired countless people who were ready to give up on life to persevere and see their life's purpose through to the end. That's how you walk out of disaster and into destiny. I've been there, and I've lived it.

I sometimes feel that it's sort of a mysterious "spiritual irony" that with as much as Diane and I were doing in the ministry, I believe the most impacting sermon we ever preached was that window of time when our congregation, family, and friends watched us never stop serving. They saw us give all glory to God right at the apex of our suffering. I know for a fact that it inspired people to stop thinking of their job as a worthless vocation and start thinking of it as a means to fulfilling purpose. And for those who discovered that their job wasn't fulfilling purpose, they stepped out in faith and found one that was.

By this point in our journey, Diane and I had gotten past "hump day" and allowed the suffering to refine our purpose on Thursday. We were preparing ourselves for Friday to be a day of making some financial decisions that were becoming an urgent necessity.

Spiritual Lifelines for Your Vocation

1. When you're going through the ordinary routine of life, it's very easy to become complacent with your vocation. Allow trials to help refine your vocation, causing you to do it better if it serves a higher purpose, and replace it if it doesn't.

2. God created you with a very specific purpose to fulfill in the earth. It's not a mysterious "some-

thing" that you have to go to a mountaintop to find. It's simply your day-by-day walk in obedience to His Word and His will for your life, irrespective of your occupation.

3. You know that you're doing your purpose when tough times cannot stop what you're doing. Severe trials can stop you for doing things for money, regardless of how much money it is, but they cannot stop you from fulfilling a purpose that's burning in your heart, that won't allow you to quit.

ENDNOTE

1. Andy Stanley, *Visioneering* (Sisters, OR: Multnomah, 1999).

SECTION VI

Friday
THE FINANCIAL

Work is about daily meaning as well as daily bread;
for recognition as well as cash; for astonishment
rather than torpor; in short, for a sort of life rather
than a Monday through Friday sort of dying. . . .
We have a right to ask of work that it include
meaning, recognition, astonishment, and life.

—STUDS TURKEL

Chapter 24

HUMBLE BEGINNINGS

Just make up your mind at the very outset that your work is going to stand for quality...that you are going to stamp a superior quality upon everything that goes out of your hands, that whatever you do shall bear the hallmark of excellence.

—ORISON SWETT MARDEN

The last thing you want to talk about with your spouse is what you need to do to get your finances in order before one of you leaves the earth. It's almost an admission that one of you is getting ready to do so. Although Diane and I had many poignant and moving discussions during her final months alive, I always avoided the "money talk." I'm actually glad that Diane handled our finances with the astute precision of a Fortune 500 accountant. She made sure all of our accounts and insurances were in order. That saved me from having to experience the guilt of doing it myself and from having to ask her some questions pertaining to mortality in the process.

I've already shared on several occasions in this book that Diane and

I both came from very humble beginnings. I believe our backgrounds led Diane and I to be not only frugal, but also resilient with respect to finances. Even after we started to have more money, Diane was always very careful with our finances and worked hard to make the most of every dollar. After she died, looking back through the detailed financial records she kept reminded me of a story from when we first met and her ability to always make something out of nothing.

Chapter 25

ANGEL IN A BLUE DRESS

Never tell people how to do things. Tell them what to do and they will surprise you with their ingenuity.

—GENERAL GEORGE S. PATTON

When it came time for the ordination for my first pastorate, Diane and I were broke, but full of ambition. I was in my early 20s and full of zeal to change the world. Through what I view now as divine orchestration, my pastor and mentor at the time decided to leave the church he was pastoring—or maybe the church decided it was time for him to go. Either way, I was working on staff as an associate pastor. Being that he was my pastor and spiritual mentor, I just assumed that if he was resigning or getting a pink slip, so was I.

To my surprise, the church's leadership wanted me to take over as senior pastor! Even more surprising, my pastor actually wanted me to stay behind and accept the position. It was an overwhelming transition, but one eased by Diane's constant encouragement. Although Diane knew how elaborate the ordination service would be, she wasn't quite prepared to go out and buy a Donna Karan evening gown for the occasion. Instead, she went to Wal-Mart, bought some fabric, and sewed herself a beautiful blue dress. The dress was magnificent, and the ordination was a wonderful celebration. Most significantly, Diane's actions were a pure example of her can-do attitude.

It's funny (well, it's not really funny), but I was thinking about that dress from Wal-Mart when it was about time to speak with Diane about our finances. After she had attended her last service at the church in December 2004, Diane's health rapidly declined. I knew she was tired, and I found out she had signed a DNR ("Do Not Resuscitate") order at the hospital. My heart broke, but I knew her departure was close at hand. And it was time to have the talk.

If you have not been one who has been well-trained when it comes to managing money, purpose to begin that training now so that the state of your finances will help, rather than hinder, your future.

We were fortunate enough to have some basic understanding of money because we lived in the same city as best-selling financial expert Dave Ramsey and considered him a friend. A passage from one of his books best describes the importance of understanding the relationship between money and your life and the necessity of being financially competent—especially in situations like ours.

> First, money is active. Finances and money are always moving. Time, interest rates, amounts, cash flows, inflation and risk all intermingle to create a current that is ever flowing. Whether you choose to impact these currents is irrelevant, they still go on. If you took $10,000 and buried it in the backyard for ten years, will it buy as much when you dig it up as it will now? Obviously not. We must learn that the current or flow of the mathematical process is always affecting our money. It never stops. Money in this sense is like a beautiful thoroughbred horse—very powerful and always in action, but unless this horse is trained when very young, it will be an out-of-control and dangerous animal when it grows to maturity. The point is this: You must gain control over your money or the lack of it will forever control you.[1]

If you have not been one who has been well-trained when it comes to managing money, purpose to begin that training now so that the state of your finances will help, rather than hinder, your future.

ENDNOTE

1.   Dave Ramsey, *Financial Peace Revisited* (New York: Viking Penguin, 2003).

Chapter 26

BITTERSWEET DISCOVERIES

In peace, as a wise man, he should make suitable
preparation for war.

—HORACE

Talking with Diane about our finances was bittersweet because on the one hand, I found out that she pretty much had everything in order. On the other hand, "everything in order" meant things were set up financially for me to go on alone. While it was a very painful time, I do believe that the important financial items that we discussed in depth will help you to get your own finances in order. Here are the things we talked through that I believe will be of great benefit to your life:

Our Home—Diane and I owned a home together. As a young couple we started out in an apartment, but our goal was always to own a home. We accomplished that goal. If you own a home, that's excellent. If not, begin taking steps toward home ownership now. It could end up being the one major asset you leave to the next generation.

Our Insurance—Diane made sure we had all of the necessary insurances in place (life, health, home, automobile, etc.). Insurance is never cheap, and most of us hate paying the premiums. However, I believe that if you own a nice car with a luxury payment, it's better to buy a used car and allocate that car payment toward some life insurance and health insurance for your family.

Our Will—We had a will. I'm not talking about my ability to choose here. I'm talking about a legal document that says what's going to happen after you die. This is not an expensive document to create. Get it done now instead of leaving it up to the state to decide what happens to your stuff.

Our Savings—Since Diane was always so frugal, she made sure that we had a savings account set up and that money was going into it on a regular basis. Open a savings account, and set up with your employer to automatically put a certain amount from your check into that account. That way, you won't even miss it.

Although it tore my heart out, it was also quite a relief to have this discussion with Diane. Instead of agonizing over money, we simply had to set up a plan of action for dealing with our mortality and the finality of her illness. But who wants to talk about finances on a Friday? Diane and I both were ready to get beyond that discussion and that day so we could wake up Saturday morning and reminisce about our wonderful relationship with each other and the great ones we shared with others.

Spiritual Lifelines for Your Finances

1. After reading this book, make your next priority analyzing your financial situation. Even if you're starting with no money or in debt, make a

conscious decision to get your will and your insurance coverage (health, home, automobile, life) in place.

2. Don't wait for a tragedy to deal with your finances. Tragedy comes to all of our lives at one time or another. Make it easier on yourself and your loved ones by getting your finances in order now.

3. Don't think of money as a means of immediate gratification. Although Diane and I never had kids, we were always thinking generationally with our finances. You should do the same. Think about your children and your grandchildren. What type of legacy will you leave, one of indebtedness, or one of freedom and prosperity?

SECTION VII

Saturday
THE RELATIONAL

Satire is what closes on Saturday night.
—GEORGE S. KAUFMAN

Chapter 27

PRINCETON OVER PRIDE

Forgiveness is the answer to the child's dream of a miracle by which what is broken is made whole again, what is soiled is again made clean.

—DAG HAMMARSKJOLD

The word *satire* is defined as a "spoof or caricature of something; a parody." Satire is what happens on *Saturday Night Live.* After the week that Diane and I had experienced, we almost felt like the tragedy of it all bordered on the edge of hilarity. We needed to be able to laugh about something—or at least smile. The two things that brought a smile to both of our faces were talking about our relationship and reminiscing about memorable times with family and friends. That's why I think that it's fitting here to share a few stories that Diane and I thought back on as Saturday night came to a close. It's my hope that sharing these stories will inspire you to consider your own interpersonal relationships and do everything you can to improve them now before it's too late.

Diane and I were both overly ambitious by nature, and sometimes that led to mini skirmishes. From the early 1990s on, I was in a zone, working hard to build the ministry, while Diane pursued her dream of being a doctor. To say that we were both strong-willed and fiercely determined to succeed would be an understatement. Relentless is probably a much better adjective to describe our quests.

We were both invigorated by a divine mandate that compelled us to love each other deeply, but one that could also ignite some serious tensions when we didn't agree on something. I distinctly remember one argument we had. We were still in the midst of the resolution process when I left for some appointments that morning. While I was gone that day, lo and behold, a letter arrived in the mail announcing that I had been accepted to Princeton to pursue a doctorate degree. Diane was still so mad at me from our argument (as she later told me) that she thought about destroying the letter before I got home. I think guilt got the best of her. Tempers cooled, I got the letter, and we made up and rejoiced together. I commuted between Nashville and New Jersey for a couple of years and earned that Princeton doctorate.

That story is only funny now because she didn't actually destroy the letter before I saw it. Had she done so, I probably would have eventually discovered I had been accepted to Princeton anyway, but the damage of her actions might have caused an irreparable breach in our relationship.

I'm so glad the breach was repaired and our relationship flourished. Diane was a bridge builder by nature, so she always seemed to be working hard to prepare broken relationships. I think that's one of the reasons she hated divorce so much. She felt like a bridge had been torn apart every time she learned of a couple determining to separate.

Being a bridge builder is also one of the things that caused Diane to repair the breaches in her own family. We all know how hard it can be to mend family relationships. Most of us just leave them alone, and don't bother to even seek reconciliation. I love how Diane always took the opposite approach and moved toward aggressive restoration of family relationships.

Chapter 28

MEND THE CIRCLE

What breaks in a moment may take years to mend.
—SWEDISH PROVERB

Family relationships are like using a pen to outline a circle. Regardless of which way you go, you always end up coming back at the same starting point—face-to-face with a family member. I think God did that on purpose, so we wouldn't be so quick to dismiss a family member over a simple disagreement or difference of opinion.

Diane had an uncommon relationship with her older sister Dalre while growing up. Since their father was absent and her mother worked long hours, Dalre was more like a second mom than a big sister. We all know that moms and daughters don't always see eye-to-eye. Diane and Dalre certainly had their share of disagreements. But it was interesting to watch Diane mend the circle of their relationship after she reached adulthood. I think Diane realized that Dalre, more than trying to be her mother, was really just attempting to shield and protect her little sister from the harshness of the world.

If you've got some family relationships that are cracked, make an effort to mend the broken places. Sometimes it's just a simple acknowledgment that you're not always *right.*

Out of this revelation grew a relationship that turned into a BFF (Best Friends Forever) relationship. But Diane refused to let the mending stop with just her relationship with her sister Dalre. Even though her dad had abandoned the family while she was still a child, Diane made sure that things were right between the two of them before he died.

If you've got some family relationships that are cracked, make an effort to mend the broken places. Sometimes it's just a simple acknowledgment that you're not *always* right. Throughout Diane's illness Dalre was one of her closest confidants. You never know whom you may need to call on, both in sickness and in health. Reach out to someone today and mend the circle.

Chapter 29

FORGIVENESS AT SUNSET

Accept the pain, cherish the joys, resolve the regrets; then can come the best of benedictions— "If I had my life to live over, I'd do it all the same."
—JOAN MCINTOSH

If you've ever had the chance to catch a glimpse of the sun just as it's slipping over the horizon, you know that it's like a huge mirror reflecting a message back to you: *This day is done. Gone is the sun. For a thousand tomorrows, I rise.* What an amazing phrase, *This day is done!* And who can tell the sun that it's wrong, or ask it to wait a few more minutes?

We all have circumstances in our lives that have run their course and are rapidly approaching sunset. For some, your very life is nearing sunset. The beautiful thing about forgiveness is that, like the sun, it brings warmth, growth, and healing. And most importantly, it keeps on giving those things for a thousand tomorrows.

Diane's father walked out on the family when she was nine. When he left, he took all of his love—and his emotional and financial support—with him, never sharing it with Diane or her siblings. Decades later, when Diane's father's life was slipping over the horizon, she decided to share the gift of forgiveness. Diane flew down to Jackson, Mississippi, made amends and cared for her father during the last weeks of his life. What a beautiful sunset.

Watching Diane forgive her father literally made me reach out to some of my own family members with a restorative tone. I was awed at Diane's ability to not only to forgive but to always be thinking of others even in the midst of the overwhelming pain she was experiencing.

If there's someone you need to forgive, do it today before that life, or yours, slips over the horizon.

Chapter 30

PARTY LIKE IT'S 1999

A man is called selfish, not for pursuing his own
good, but for neglecting his neighbor's.
—RICHARD WHATELY

Have you ever just made up your mind that you were going to throw a surprise party for someone else? If it's someone who's really close to you, it can be excruciatingly difficult to secretly put together a list, create invites, and gather all of the necessities for creating a memorable event. It often becomes more of a covert operation than simply a secret gathering of friends and loved ones to surprise the intended person of honor. But it's always the emotion written all over the person's face (delight, awe, embarrassment, warmth) that makes the occasion and all that led up to it worthwhile.

Diane had such a party in mind for her sister Dalre in 2004. She worked in the shadows with her cousin, Vanessa, and pulled everything together just in time for the big day. And boy, was Dalre surprised and overcome with emotion! More so than just getting the special attention on her birthday, Dalre was so touched because Diane pulled all of this

169

together from her hospital bed, two months before she died when she was at her weakest. In fact, the festivities took place right there in the hospital room. Diane laughed, cried, and joked that day like it was 1999 (1999, when she was healthy and disease-free).

Think of someone today that you can honor, maybe even a stranger or acquaintance, and throw him or her a party like it's 1999.

Think of someone today that you can honor, maybe even a stranger or acquaintance, and throw him or her a party like it's 1999.

Chapter 31

MIDNIGHT

I stood on the bridge at midnight, As the clocks
were striking the hour.
—HENRY WADSWORTH LONGFELLOW

Near the very end of Diane's life there were times when I wished
more than anything that we could go back to 1999. If God gave
me the opportunity to go back and choose our life's direction with the
options being His good will, His acceptable will, and His perfect will,
the good would be Diane having acid reflux instead of cancer. The
acceptable would be the doctor finding a tumor, but finding it early
enough to operate and remove it. And the perfect would be Diane
having never been sick at all.

In the final weeks of Diane's life I didn't want to leave her side, but
when I did, I kept my phone on vibrate and made sure it was touching
my body at all times. That way whether I was in the pulpit or in the car,
I would not miss her call.

Diane always wanted me to take a Sunday off to just rest and
recover, but I would never do it. Her last gift to me was a Sunday off.

Early Sunday morning on January 16, 2005, while I was getting a couple of hours of sleep before heading to the church, my phone rang. It was the hospital calling to tell me I needed to get over there right away. Instead of preaching three sermons that Sunday morning, I spent seven beautiful hours with my beloved Diane before she slipped into eternity at 11:00 A.M.

After a long and arduous week, it was finally time to rest. Together, Diane and I had journeyed through the spiritual, soulful, physical, educational, vocational, financial, and relational aspects of our lives—and I was richer for it. It's my prayer that your life is now richer too.

May this story that's dear to my heart empower, encourage, and inspire you to live your "best week" now, regardless of what life may bring your way *between Sundays.*

SECTION VIII

THE TRUTH IN THE DARK

All truths are easy to understand once they are discovered; the point is to discover them.

—GALILEO

Chapter 32

WHEN YOU'RE DOWN TO NOTHING, GOD IS UP TO SOMETHING

The Lord gets His best soldiers out of the highlands of affliction.

—CHARLES HADDON SPURGEON

Through the course of my life I have discovered that when you are down to nothing God is up to something. No person is immune to affliction, even a child of God. However, the child of God has a perspective on life that the unbeliever does not have. As a believer in God you view your reality differently than other people. When other people give up on you and write you off, you know that in the face of their pessimism God is up to something. God is at His best when faced with human impossibilities. When we are at our lowest, it's God's opportunity to act on our behalf. When we are in that difficult place, like I was during Diane's illness, we may not be able to see what He is up to, but eventually we will come to the place where we can see how

God was working behind the scenes on our behalf. The Bible is full of stories that exemplify this dynamic truth.

In the Old Testament there is a story about a widow and a prophet (see 1 Kings 17). The widow is down to her last meal. In preparation she goes out to gather a few sticks to make a fire for the final meal for her and her son. You cannot get lower than this. As she is gathering sticks the prophet Elijah shows up. Elijah isn't doing much better either. He is in a war against Ahab and Jezebel, the king and queen. By the word of the Lord Elijah tells Ahab that drought is coming and will not be broken except by the prophet's word. God tells Elijah to go to the brook Cherith and there he will find water and ravens will feed him. This comfortable spot did not last very long. Because of the drought the brook finally dried up and there was no more water for him.

Here is where the story gets really interesting. God tells the prophet Elijah to go to Zarephath and there he will find a widow who will provide for him. This is the same widow who is getting ready to prepare a final meal for her and her son. Elijah meets the widow at the gate of the city and asks her for some water. Not knowing that he is a prophet, she heads to the local well to get him a drink. When she turns to go get the water Elijah asks her to also bring him some food. Remember that God is the One who has set up this encounter. He knows the widow has no food. But this meeting will lead to a divine intervention for her.

The widow is down to nothing and the prophet asks her for something. She tells the prophet that she was about to make a cake for her and her son. After their last meal, they are going to have the last drink and then they are going to die. This is no ordinary widow. In the face of potential starvation she is willing to share her last meal with the prophet. Her hospitality opened the door for a miracle. Standing in the kitchen using up the last of her flour, she prepares what she thinks is her final meal. But she discovers that she still has flour and oil for more. The ingredients for the meal never run out.

God is pretty good at multiplying food and drink when everything has run out and your pantry is empty. The first miracle that Jesus ever performed was at a wedding where the wine ran out. Horrified, His mother Mary told the servants to do whatever Jesus would tell them to do. We all remember how He turned the water into wine (see John 2:1-11).

On another occasion Jesus had tried to get away from the crowds (not an easy thing to do for the One who works miracles) and ended up going up a mountain near the Sea of Galilee (see Matt. 14:13-21). Well, the crowds always found Him. He looked out at the growing throng of cripples, blind people, and those who had lost their hearing. As always, His compassion trumped His physical weariness and He began to minister to the sick. For three days He ministered to the mass of 5,000 people.

On the third day He saw that they were beginning to get weak from hunger. In typical Jesus style, He told His disciples to feed them. Stunned by His words, they asked Him how they were going to feed so many people. Jesus had them gather up all the food that they could and told them to bring the food to Him. They returned with a measly five loaves and two fish. Without a pause, Jesus held up the food and blessed it and then told His disciples to feed the crowd with these provisions. To their amazement they fed the whole swarm of people with these meager provisions. When they were down to nothing, God was up to something.

I know that some of you reading this book right now have experienced being down to your last dime and wondering when God would show up. To your surprise God stepped in with a miracle. While your money was running out, God was planning a surprise for you. You are still here this very day because God was up to something for your life.

Don't you give up because your friends have become few and your enemies have become new! Don't you give up because your money is funny and your life has turned to strife. This is not the time to be depressed nor discouraged because you need to know that when you're down to nothing, God is up to something.

Life does not always work out the way we think it will. Your dreams may have turned into nightmares, but you need to understand God is at His best when your back is up against the wall and you don't know which way to turn. You are in the perfect place for a miracle.

> *Although the fig tree shall not blossom, neither shall fruit be in the vines; the labor of the olive shall fail, and the fields shall yield no meat; the flock shall be cut off from the fold, and there shall be no herd in the stalls: Yet I will rejoice in the Lord, I will joy in the God of my salvation. The Lord God is my strength, and He will make my feet like hinds' feet, and He will make me to walk upon mine high places. To the chief singer on my stringed instruments* (Habakkuk 3:17-19 KJV).

The prophet Habakkuk penned these compelling words in the middle of the seventh century B.C. There is no biographical information on the prophet Habakkuk; in fact less is known about him than any other writer of the Bible. Although his name does not appear in any other part of the Jewish Bible, Rabbinic tradition holds that Habakkuk was the Shunammite woman's son, who was restored to life by Elisha. Due to the liturgical nature of the Book of Habakkuk, some scholars think that the author may have been a temple prophet.

This verse was probably written in a time of great trial in Habakkuk's own life. His declaration is spoken with great resolve. There is nothing that will cause him to lose the song of the Lord. Even if he should lose everything that would provide him a good life, he will not give in to doubt or depression. Even if there is nothing going right in my life—nothing in my barn, nothing in my fields, and everything is falling apart—I will sing the Lord's song in a difficult time.

SINGING IN THE PAIN

Although the fig tree shall not blossom, neither shall fruit be in the vines; the labor of the olive shall fail, and the fields shall yield no meat; the flock shall be cut off from the fold, and there shall be no herd in the stalls (Habakkuk 3:17 KJV).

This is the first lesson that the prophet wants to communicate. There are times and seasons in every life when life will overwhelm you. The prophet says that at those times God will preserve you in your pain. Many of you have wondered where is God when it hurts. I am here today to tell you that God has not forsaken you. God will defend you and maintain you in your darkest hour. Regardless of the extent of your pain, it is God who keeps watch over your life. When you've lost your job He is there. When you are struck by cancer He will not leave you. When others have abandoned you He will not forsake you. When there is not enough money to pay your next mortgage payment, He will make a way for you where there seems to be no way. It is in those moments, when you are walking through the dark night of the soul, that you must hang on to God and His Word.

When you think things are going down, God is coming up... with a plan for your recovery. The fact that you can still sing in the midst of sorrow is an indication that God is getting through to you.

The prophet said that in the face of failure he would still rejoice. He would put his joy, not in his circumstances, but in the God who stands above his circumstances. There is a big difference between joy and happiness. Happiness is based upon happenings. Happiness is produced in your life when things are going right. Joy is based upon something more profound and impenetrable. It is based upon revelation. Happiness is based upon what we see. Joy is based upon what we cannot see. It is based upon a revelation that comes from a different realm. That revelation gives us strength in the midst of our sorrow and

181

causes us to sing when all is crumbling around us.

Mahatma Gandhi was one who suffered much for the independence of India. In reflecting on his pain he wrote, "Joy lies in the fight, in the attempt, in the suffering involved, not in the victory itself."[1] Gandhi learned what many of us have discovered. Vision and revelation empower us in the midst of our struggles. When we lift up our eyes from the shadows of our situation and look upon the Lord, our hearts will be encouraged and a new song will be given.

I serve a God who neither sleeps nor slumbers. He watches over Israel, and I know He watches over me. I serve a God who makes sure that when my enemies and my foes come to eat at my flesh they will stumble and fall. I serve a God who will supply every last one of my needs according to His riches and glory. I serve a God who is my Shepherd and I shall not want. It does not matter what the landscape of my life looks like, I still have a joy on the inside of me. As the old Gospel song goes: "This joy I have, the world didn't give it and the world can't take it away."

Who kept you through the storm? Who kept you through the rain? Who kept you when you didn't know which way you were going to go? "God kept you in the midst of your pain." When you had no power, no money, when all of life seemed to deny you of any hope, God was there! Yes, there are times when dark clouds cast their shadows over our lives, but those dark clouds are never permanent. The brightness of God's presence will always drive away those intimidating clouds.

You should not fear the power of the night. The night creates new songs for us to sing. St. John of the Cross, a Catholic saint who endured great hardship throughout his life, discovered this truth of the darkness that leads to the light. Hundreds of years ago he penned these words:

> *In the happy night,*
> *In secret, when none saw me,*
> *Nor I beheld aught,*
> *Without light or guide, save that which burned in*
> *   my heart.*

This light guided me
More surely than the light of noonday
To the place where he (well I knew who!) was awaiting
  me—
A place where none appeared.

Oh, night that guided me,
Oh, night more lovely than the dawn,
Oh, night that joined Beloved with lover,
Lover transformed in the Beloved![2]

POWER TO THE POWERLESS

In the midst of a severe situation St. John declared that the Lord God is his strength. What he is saying is, "When I was powerless, He gave me power." In the midst of the dark places, emotional trauma, and financial stress you must know where your strength is. There are times in our lives when we all feel the pain of powerless. No matter how you try to mask your misfortune and conceal your chaos, the pain drains away your reservoir of strength. It feels like at any moment you're going to lose control of your emotions and succumb to the encroaching trouble in your life.

It is in these moments that you understand you must tap into a higher power. You must put God in a place of dominion in your life. You don't have the power or the wisdom to prevail over the impending doom that seeks to cloud God's glory in your life. Your response is a *cry*—a cry for help from the One who has all power. As you lift your eyes above your circumstances you now understand that the "is-ness" of God will overcome what "isn't" in your life. As long as God *is*—you're not—the "is-ness" of God is the yes of God. The yes of God is always louder than the no of the enemy. It doesn't matter how many no's I run into, as long as I know that God is. "I am what I am" is the most powerful revelation of the nature of God. It reveals God as the ever-present One who is sufficient to resolve any situation in your life. When you are knocked down by the troubling circumstances of your life, it is the Lord God who will pick you up and cause you to stand on the Rock.

When you are questioning *Who in the world can help me and how in the world can I escape this maze?*, the answer begins to reverberate in your spirit: The Lord is. *Who in the world is going to heal my body?* The Lord is. *Who in the world is going to make a way out of no way?* The Lord is. When you put Him over you, you come under the power of His will. In those moments you discover that the Lord is your Shepherd. The song of David now becomes your song:

> *The Lord is my shepherd,*
> *I shall not be in want* [I lack nothing].
> *He makes me lie down in green pastures,*
> *He leads me beside quiet waters,*
> *He restores* [refreshes] *my soul.*
> *He guides me in paths of righteousness* [along the right
>   paths] *for His name's sake.*
>
> *Even though I walk* [through the darkest valley]
>   *through the valley of the shadow of death,*
> *I will fear no evil,*
> *for You are with me;*
> *Your rod and Your staff,*
> *they comfort me.*
>
> *You prepare a table before me in the presence of my*
>   *enemies.*
> *You anoint my head with oil;*
> *my cup overflows.*
>
> *Surely* [Your] *goodness and love will follow me all the*
>   *days of my life,*

and I will dwell in the house of the Lord forever
(Psalm 23).

Yes, you will walk through dark valleys. Yes, you will face the enemy. But in those moments the promise of His presence is always there. Even if it looks like you *don't* have, you know it doesn't mean that you *won't* have!

The Lord is over—in other words, because He is over everything He can work it all out. He's over your debt. He's over your sickness. He's over your depression. He is over your feelings of rejection. Whatever I'm going through, God sits above. When you understand this, it gives you a greater sense of determination, because now you understand that you are not alone. There is One who will supply force to your frailty, forgiveness for your failure, and calm to your confusion.

Your determination and willingness to hang in there is not based upon your power but upon His. When you relinquish your place and submit to His will, a passageway is opened up that allows the "all of God" to flow into your life. You can now face the dangers of life because of the assurance that you've got Somebody up there who's working and taking care of your life.

One of the great prophets of Israel captured this revelation of God when he wrote these words:

> *Hast thou not known? hast thou not heard, that the ever-lasting God, the Lord, the Creator of the ends of the earth, fainteth not, neither is weary? there is no searching of His understanding. He giveth power to the faint; and to them that have no might He increaseth strength. Even the youths shall faint and be weary, and the young men shall utterly fall: But they that wait upon the Lord shall renew their strength; they shall mount up with wings as eagles; they shall run, and not be weary; and they shall walk, and not faint* (Isaiah 40:28-31 KJV).

GOD IS PRESERVING YOU FOR HIS PURPOSES

"...**He will make** my feet like hinds' feet, and **He will make** me to walk upon mine high places..." (Hab. 3:19 KJV). *God* "will make. ..." The focus is on what God will do, not what you can do. God is always up to something even when you cannot see His actions. You must understand that everything God allowed to happen in your life has a purpose. Everything you've been through, you didn't realize it had a purpose. Life is not easy, but as Madame Curie said we must persevere until we discover the purpose:

> Life is not easy for any of us. But what of that? We must have perseverance and above all confidence in ourselves. We must believe that we are gifted for something, and that this thing, at whatever cost, must be attained.[3]

In the midst of your perseverance God is preserving you for His purposes. Every single event in your life has a purpose. Because all things work together for good for those who love God and are called according to His purpose (see Rom. 8:28). If you're in the will of God, the good, the bad, the ups, the downs are all working together. I will admit that while we are walking through the dark night of the soul it does not look like it is working out for good. In the dark places our vision is blurred so that we cannot see the wider picture. But I am sure that all of us can say that as we look back we finally are able to see clearly and know that God was there all the time. His apparent silence was only an illusion of absence. When I look back over my life and some of the things I've gone through, I confidently say, "Lord, I want to thank You, because now I realize how these things have ultimately blessed me."

While you thought you were going down, God was in the process of promoting you. Some of you don't realize that right now you're in a process of promotion. If you don't go through this, you won't get where God's trying to take you. If you don't survive this, you're not going to walk into the promise of God. When you're down to nothing, God is up to something. And that something is a good thing.

God knows that character must be built into your life. God knows that character is formed under pressure. In the midst of the pressure the life of God is formed in you preparing you for the next level of promotion that is coming to your life. God knew that the character you needed for the next dimension in your life could only come by going through the dark valley. In the valley He gives you hind's feet so that you can climb the mountains. God makes my feet like hinds' feet because hinds' feet are necessary to get to the highest levels. We must make the prayer of Peter Marshall, former Chaplain of the U.S. Senate, our prayer: "When we long for life without difficulties, remind us that oaks grow strong in contrary winds and diamonds are made under pressure."

When you are going through tough times, the enemy seeks to confuse you and convince you that God does not love you and that your destiny is to wallow in the slough of despondency and the mire of anonymity. What you must understand is that the trouble you are walking through is a pathway to your purpose. The trail that was leading you to your destiny had to pass by the way of pain. Your final destination was not found in the words of Habakkuk 3:17, but in the dynamic prose found in verse 19. Though the darkness surrounds you, God makes you walk. Though you fall, He picks you up. Though your strength fails, He gives His strength. God has a destiny for your life and He will walk with you, leading you to that perfect place. The low places are not your final destiny. God has built you to live in the high places, and that is where you are headed.

Even to this day I love getting a rubber band and a paper clip and shooting the paper clip into the air. Once while I was shooting paper clips, God spoke to me and said, "The greater the tension, the greater the pull; and the greater the pull, the higher the paper clip will go." This is the revelation of the rubber band. Tension creates power, and that power will launch us into higher places.

When you are at the end of your own strength, when you are down to nothing, God is up to something!

ENDNOTES

1.   Mahatma Gandhi, accessed at: http://thinkexist.com/ quotations/joy.

2.   St. John of the Cross (1542–1591), "Stanzas of the Soul," accessed at: http://www.ccel.org/ccel/john_cross/dark_night.html.

3.   Marie Curie, accessed at: http://thinkexist.com/ quotation/life_is_not_easy_for_any_of_us-but_what_of_that/ 9171 .html.

Chapter 33

A WORD IN YOUR WILDERNESS

Be careful to follow every command I am giving you today, so that you may live and increase and may enter and possess the land that the Lord promised on oath to your forefathers. Remember how the Lord your God led you all the way in the desert these forty years, to humble you and to test you in order to know what was in your heart, whether or not you would keep His commands. He humbled you, causing you to hunger and then feeding you with manna, which neither you nor your fathers had known, to teach you that man does not live on bread alone but on every word that comes from the mouth of the Lord. Your clothes did not wear out and your feet did not swell during these forty years.

Observe the commands of the Lord your God, walking in His ways and revering Him. For the Lord your God is bringing you into a good land—a land with streams and pools of water, with springs flowing in the valleys and hills; a land with wheat and barley, vines and fig trees, pomegranates, olive oil and honey; a land where bread will not be scarce and you will lack nothing; a land where the rocks are iron and you can dig copper out of the hills.

But remember the Lord your God, for it is He who gives you the ability to produce wealth, and so confirms His covenant, which He swore to your fore-fathers, as it is today (Deuteronomy 8:1-4;6-9;18).

It is God's desire to bring us out of places of oppression and bondage and to deliver us into places of promise and destiny. God does this by requiring His people to obey His voice. Throughout the Scriptures we are reminded of the power of obedience in accessing the promises of the Lord. From Genesis to Revelation we see evidence of the link between obedience and promise.

The Book of Deuteronomy is the last book in the Pentateuch, the Law of Moses. These books give us the beginning of the history of Israel and the law that would eventually govern their world. It is a word that comes out of the wilderness. Its message is clear. If you do not walk right and you choose the way of wickedness, you will delay the process of coming into your ultimate destiny. But if you choose to obey the voice of the Lord, that decision will lead you to the place where the promises of God will be fulfilled and your destiny will be found.

Life is about choices, and the choices we make have great impact upon the direction of our lives. God gave us a great gift when He gave us the power of free will. But with that gift comes great responsibility. Empowered by free will, we have the opportunity to determine our destiny.

Righteousness is often interpreted as a harsh and difficult word in a culture that is adrift in an ocean of existential humanism and moral confusion. Humanity has lost its way because it has forgotten the word given in the wilderness—a word meant to guide us through our lives. When we ignore the Word of the Lord we open ourselves to be led into wrong places, far from the purpose of God for our lives. It is only when we return to the Word of the Lord and begin to obey the Word that we will find our way back to the path designed for us. It is only through unwavering obedience to divine truth that we can survive in the midst of a postmodern society that denies the truth of that Word.

Israel is a powerful example of this truth. Israel was to be God's community on the earth, reflecting His reality and character. Delivered from Egypt the Israelites found themselves in the wilderness. As we all know, the wilderness is not our destiny. It is only a passageway to the promised land of our destiny. But, as we learn from the history of Israel, the possibility exists of spending more time in the wilderness than we should. The reason why it took the Israelites many years to come out of what was supposed to be a short, few days' journey was because of their disobedience.

But here is the good news: in the midst of Israel's disobedience, God does not wipe them out. He gives them a principle, a word that will lead them out of the place of disobedience. In other words, God is patient with them until they're able to graduate to a place to be released into their destiny.

Similarly, God covers us until His power can heal us. Even when we abandon Him, He does not leave us as orphans. He is the good Father who remains with us even when we do not deserve it.

The word on obedience is a word about choices, choosing to take God's Word and make it more important than our word. Sometimes the smallest decisions that you make produce the greatest results. You can never minimize any decision you make. I have discovered that it is not difficult to make decisions when you know what your values are. When you make the way of righteousness your determination then it will make your decisions much easier. Sometimes your choices will alienate you from others but never be afraid to walk alone when you have made the right choice.

God said "every" commandment. We are responsible for every commandment that God has given. Each commandment contains a promise of a full life if we only hold fast to that word. We are not given the option of selective obedience. Obeying God is not like a trip to the grocery store where we pick and choose what we like. We are commanded to walk in all the commandments of God. These commandments are given for our protection. They are placed before us as a guide for directing our lives. These commands will sometimes stretch us, but when the linings of our soul have been stretched they will never return to their undersized place. We are stretched by the Word of the Lord so that we can better contain the glory of God.

Sometimes the smallest decisions that you make produce the greatest results. You can never minimize any decision you make. I have discovered that it is not difficult to make decisions when you know what your values are.

Obedience is a calculated choice to comply and to carry out the will of God for your life. We are not born with an automatic instinct to obey. We live in a culture that emphasizes selfishness and humanistic determination. Obedience is something that is learned in the processes of life. All of our experiences offer to us opportunities to learn what it means to obey God.

MAKE OBEDIENCE TO GOD YOUR PRIORITY

If you're going to walk in obedience you have to accept that God must be the most important person in your life; He has to be your priority. If God does not have first place in your life then you will not be able to obey Him. Obedience must be reflected as a primary priority in your life. Obedience is not a sermon we preach but a life that we live. *Obedience is the life that we live between Sundays.*

I am not saying that obedience is easy. There are times when obedience will require that we act when we don't totally understand the totality and implications of what we being asked to do. Let me explain it this way. When we are young and our parents tell us, "Don't play in the streets" or "Go clean your room," we might not understand why. Our life experiences are not broad enough to understand why we must obey.

Similarly, when we are told to meditate on God's Word day and night, we might not fully comprehend the importance of that command. But when we get into a difficult place and don't know where to turn, the very Word that has been buried in our spirit will become the Word that will guide us through those times. We won't be susceptible to the deceiving words of the enemy. When the enemy comes and whispers in our ear, "Hath God said...?" we will know that his words are dark words of deception seeking to lead us away from the very place of protection.

The Word given in the wilderness must be a priority in your life even when you do not understand it. Through your choices you must bring down imaginations and every high thing that exalts itself against the knowledge of God (see 2 Cor. 10:5). Why? So that you can obey under pressure.

The awesome thing about God is that with the command He gives a grace to obey the command. There are times when I know I don't have it all to obey, but God gives me grace to obey. I know that in myself I

193

do not have the power to obey God. I know that my selfish soul is always crying out for its way. But I have discovered a power in the grace of God that enables me to obey all that He has commanded me.

BECOME PROFICIENT IN THE WORD

In order to obey God's Word, we must become proficient in that Word. We cannot obey what we do not know! This is why the enemy attempts to keep you from the Word. If the enemy can keep you from the Word, then he knows that your life will be surrounded by confusion. This is why Paul told Timothy:

> *All Scripture is God-breathed and is useful for teaching, rebuking, correcting and training in righteousness, so that the man of God may be thoroughly equipped for every good work* (2 Timothy 3:16-17).

God's Word is the ultimate power. In the beginning was the Word. At the sounding of that Word, time was born and a world was created. The space of our surroundings and the essence of our existence were created by the Word. It is this same Word that gives power to our lives and direction for our journey. So we must make it our priority to become proficient in that Word.

I believe you are reading this because you want the unadulterated, unedited Word of God for your life. The words of God give you insight into the nature of God. As you grow in your understanding of who God is, you will grow in your love for Him and will begin to make His Word the priority of your life.

It is sad to say that we've become proficient in everything else but the Word of God. We spend more time reading self-help books than in reading the one Book that can really help us. It is important to be proficient in your vocation. But it is also important to be proficient in the most important thing in the world: the Word of God. It is the Word that will guide you through the wilderness and console you in your sorrow.

Biology is important. It is valuable to know how our bodies work, but it is more important to know the One who created our bodies. Astronomy is a gateway to the universe and very fascinating, but it is more important to know the One who created the universe.

Listen, you can know biology, which is the study of life, but you've got to know the One who is life. You can study the great philosophers, from Socrates to Sartre, but it is more important to study the One who gave us the ultimate philosophy. You can study other languages, but what good is that if you do not know the heavenly language?

Here is a very important point: we don't study the Word just to get knowledge. Knowledge by itself will not save us. We can study the Word and yet not know the Word. The reason we study the Word is to know the will of God. The Word of God reveals to us the will of God. When we discover the will of God then we must be prepared to obey that will. The ultimate goal of knowing the Word is that I might obey what I know to do. This is the Word becoming flesh. Jesus is the ultimate example of this truth. He was the incarnate Word and declared that He only did what He saw the Father doing. Jesus was the Word that became flesh so that our flesh might become the Word. That's why the Scripture says, "Do not merely listen to the word, and so deceive yourselves. Do what it says" (James 1:22).

It is easy to listen to the Word being preached on Sunday mornings, but it is much more difficult to obey that Word between Sundays. It is easy to obey God when we are around the right people, but when those who oppose that very Word surround us, how do we behave? That is the question. Our obedience to God must be demonstrated outside the church building. It is in the marketplace where our virtue must be unveiled.

When you become proficient in the Word, you will become passionate about the Word. Knowledge creates fire. Proficiency gives birth to passion. Life was meant to be lived with passion. That's why you've got to have a passion. What inner force lifts a person out of the mainstream of mediocrity into the lonely chase of his dream? What mysterious power is so mesmerizing that it leads one to relinquish the luxuries of life in order to respond to the lure of the unthinkable? What intriguing pursuit has the power to pull one into a circle of commitment that eliminates all other fascinations outside that ring? What sacred cause awakens a person from the slumber of indifference to pursue the scent of the impossible? This powerful force is passion.

Passionate prayer and desire will be the very thing that will help you to survive the wilderness and eventually reach your land of promise. I encourage you to pray this prayer: *"Lord, give me a pure and holy passion for Your Word. Give me a desire to know Your Word and run after You. Lord, let there be continuity in my life between what You are doing and what I am doing. Let there be consistency between what I read in the Word and how I live it out in my life."*

The wilderness is not a fun place. No one ever said walking with God would be an easy thing. The wilderness is full of dry places, scorpions, and thieves. Some people will judge you because you are walking through those lonely places. Do not give in to their accusations and questions. Remain strong in the Word that you know to be true. How do you respond? Tell them that your "present circumstances" are not your future. They are only the present. Let them watch you being sustained by the Word of the Lord. Let them be amazed by the strength you have discovered, and watch them be surprised when your future explodes into your present.

People said you would not make it, but here you are still standing true to God and His Word.

OBEDIENCE LEADS TO PRODUCTIVITY

It's not enough to survive in the wilderness; you must learn to produce in the wilderness. You live by the Word of God. In the wilderness you find a word that creates a quality of life that is beyond your wildest imagination. Jesus said that He came to give us life. This life is not human life; it is a God kind of life. He came to give you a quality of life consistent with the God whom you serve. You might not have the job you wanted. Maybe you don't have the home or car you had hoped for. But, in the face of what appears to be inconsistent with your understanding of who God is, He will give you a life worth living—a life that is not defined by the things you have but by the Person you love.

In the wilderness you can experience productivity. The wilderness is associated with barrenness and infertility; nothing is expected to grow in the desert. But the God kind of life grows even in dry places. In a place that is not conducive to productivity He will make you produce for His glory. Folks may look at you and say, "Ain't nothing going on over here." They could never be more wrong. God makes things happen in crazy places.

Just as God's gifts are manifested on Sunday so He wants to reveal His gifts in you between Sundays. There is no reason to allow your present circumstances to prevent you from letting His life be manifested in you. The light shines brightest in the darkness.

Your passion will produce new life in you and around you. Your obedience causes you to L-I-V-E. If you want to go where God wants you to go, you will L-I-V-E. The devil is trying to get you to go back to Egypt, the place of bondage and despair. That's just E-V-I-L (which is *live* spelled backward). Your new life produces a will to survive and causes determination to grow in the hard soil of struggle. You lift up your eyes and gaze upon what God promised you.

You must know that your seed is greater than your situation. God has planted a seed of greatness and destiny within you, and your situation cannot forfeit what God has determined to do in you and through you. He has situated you for surplus. You are placed in a position where the resources of God are greater than the deficiencies of your circumstances. You will not only live but you will multiply, you will increase. He said that He would supply all of your needs according to the riches of His glory. Obedience sets you up for blessing and increase.

Obedience creates opportunity. Opportunity comes to those who are able to endure the wilderness. Your faithfulness in the desert places will bring you to new places. Your boss could call you in and tell you that the company is downsizing and you will be laid off. You could walk out of that office thinking this is the worst day in your life. Here's what you can't see or understand: for God's child, when one door closes another opens. God could put within you the desire to own your own business. You could obey that word and launch out. God could then bless your obedience, give you favor in the marketplace, and establish that new business. But it wouldn't happen if you had never been laid off. Getting put down provides an opportunity for you to be taken up. Right there in the middle of the wilderness you can become productive. Don't allow rejection to define your life. Rise above your despair and obey the Lord!

OBEDIENCE— THE FOUNDATION FOR A PROMISE

God's Word is a covenant. There are different kinds of covenants. Some covenants are words of agreement between equals. Marriage is that kind of covenant. God's covenant is much different because it is not an agreement between equals and it is based upon the power of the One who is able to fulfill the covenant. Some covenants in the Bible are based totally upon God. God says that this is what He is going to do and nothing will stop Him. Other covenants involve human coopera- tion. In this kind of covenant God says that if we obey Him He will do what He has declared He will do.

As we saw in the first verse of Deuteronomy chapter 8, God says that if we obey all that He has commanded us to do then we will live and increase and we will enter into the promised land. God's power coupled with the Israelites' obedience was the key to the promise.

God made a covenant with Abraham. The writer of Hebrews explains to us the power of that covenant in these words.

For when God made the promise to Abraham, since He could swear by no one greater, He swore by Himself,

198

saying, "I will surely bless you and I will surely multiply you." And so, having patiently waited, he obtained the promise. For men swear by one greater than themselves, and with them an oath given as confirmation is an end of every dispute. In the same way God, desiring even more to show to the heirs of the promise the unchange- ableness of His purpose, interposed with an oath, so that by two unchangeable things in which it is impossible for God to lie, we who have taken refuge would have strong encouragement to take hold of the hope set before us (Hebrews 6:13-18 NASB).

The covenant was based upon a promise that God would multiply Abraham and bless him. Abraham held on to the word and patiently waited till he received the promise. In the same way God has made promises to us, and in order to show that His purposes do not change, He added an oath—a vow and a covenant. He fenced Himself in with a vow to keep His promises.

The promises of God are for our encouragement and hope. The promise of God is the thing that moves me out of my reality and speaks to my possibility. It says, do not become a prisoner of your right-now, but become a pursuer of your not-yet. The promise of God is founded upon the sovereignty of God. *Sovereignty* means "supreme power without any external control." Theologically, it means that God is omnipotent, all-powerful. He can do what He wants to do, when He wants to do it, how He wants to do it, and to whom He wants to do it. God has no need to explain or rationalize His actions.

From His throne above all the earth, God chooses who He wants to bless and how He will do it. God chose Israel and called them His chosen people—not a likely choice for the blessing of God. But that's God. He doesn't choose on the basis of human wisdom.

As His child, God has chosen you to be the receiver of His prom- ises. We do not determine how He blesses us; we choose simply to worship Him because He does. God has a promise for you! God wants to cause you to live, make you increase, and bring you into your destiny. This is the love of God.

> *God has a promise for you! God wants to cause you to live, make you increase, and bring you into your destiny. This is the love of God.*

But in the wisdom of God we don't get the promise at our time of choosing. God is on a different time schedule than man. Remember Abraham. The guy had to wait a long, long time before the promise came to him. David was anointed to be king of Israel, but before he became king he was chased by Saul and pursued by the Philistines. In a moment of depression and sorrow he cried out to God, "How long, O Lord? Will You forget me forever? How long will You hide Your face from me?" (Ps. 13:1 NASB).

Time defines our world. It does not define God's world. Time, in the human sense, is the dimension in which events occur in sequence. We wake up, we take a shower, we eat breakfast, we go to work, we come home, we eat supper, we relax, and then we go to bed. Tomorrow the process begins all over again. Time is a sequence of events. History is the description of the events that have taken place in time. That is our dimension.

In God's dimension there is no time. That dimension is eternity and is not defined in time/space language. The human problem happens when God speaks into our time/space world and we interpret His word according to our understanding of time. Between the promise and the reality is a process. T.S. Eliot described it best with these words.

> Between the idea
> And the reality
> Between the motion
> And the act
> Falls the Shadow.[1]

There is a shadow that exists for all of us between the ideas God has for us and the reality of their fulfillment in our lives. In those shadows we must walk patiently and obediently. In the shadow our greatest questions are "when" and "why." *Why am I going through this? When will it end?*

God's questions are "how" and "who." How am I going to fulfill My promise in you? Whom will you trust while I work on the fulfillment?

At the time that we are doing all the right things, when we are trying to serve God, trouble comes into our life and it leaves us with a question. The question is answered in the process when obedience is being developed in our life. And then comes the time when we can possess our promise.

POSSESSING THE PROMISE

In Exodus 3:16-17 (NASB), God makes a promise to the children of Israel:

> *Go and gather the elders of Israel together and say to them, "The Lord, the God of your fathers, the God of Abraham, Isaac and Jacob, has appeared to me,*

*saying, 'I am indeed concerned about you and what
has been done to you in Egypt.*

*"'So I said, I will bring you up out of the afflic-
tion of Egypt to the land of the Canaanite and the
Hittite and the Amorite and the Perizzite and the
Hivite and the Jebusite, to a land flowing with milk
and honey.'"*

God promises Israel that He will bring them up out of the land
where the Egyptians have afflicted them. Egypt represents labor
without purpose. Egypt represents bondage and oppression. Affliction,
pain, labor without purpose, waking up every day and working without
purpose, forced to do what you don't want to do—this is Egypt. Now
God says, "I'm going to bring you up out of this. And I'm going to
bring you to the land of the Canaanites, Hittites, Amorites, the
Pezzerites, the Hivites, the Jebusites, a land flowing with milk and
honey." Now here is what's interesting. God gives them this promise
while they are still in Egypt. You are locked in the movie *Groundhog
Day,* where one day is the same as the next. God says that He is going
to put an end to the labor without purpose.

God delivers the Israelites from Egypt and by a great miracle helps
them cross the Red Sea. The place of their deliverance was also the place
of their enemies' destruction. Now they run into a problem. On the
other side of their deliverance is a desert, and on the other side of that
desert someone is occupying the land of their promise.

In those moments of walking in the shadow that exists between the
promise and the reality, we must understand that there are seasons in
our life. The seasons are created for our future. As we walk through
those seasons we will eventually reach our promised land. There are
seasons when obstacles raise their ugly heads, trying to prevent us from
reaching the other side. So God says, "Listen now, remember it's about
a season."

Finally, Israel gets to the River Jordan and on the other side is their promised land. Moses chooses 12 men, a representative from each tribe, to go over and spy out the land. They go to spy out the land to see the promise they were given in Exodus 3:17, to see what would become their possession.

The spies return, and we are all familiar with the two grossly different reports. A group of ten men could only see the obstacles. They saw the giants and their hearts were afraid. They were only common laborers. How could they defeat these giants? They saw themselves as grasshoppers in the sight of these giants. Their vision of themselves was a perverted vision. They could not see that the God within them was stronger than the giants in the land. Because Israel believed the reports of the spies rather than the word of the Lord, they would have to return to the desert so that they could see with the eyes of God.

In Joshua chapter 1, which takes place about 40 years later, Israel is back again at the same river looking at the same land that was still full of giants and walled cities. Before Moses died, he left these words with them:

> *Now it shall be, if you diligently obey the Lord your God, being careful to do all His commandments which I command you today, the Lord your God will set you high above all the nations of the earth* (Deuteronomy 28:1 NASB).

This time they are ready to obey the word of the Lord and possess the land. In the silence of the moment Joshua hears the word of the Lord:

> *Moses My servant is dead; now therefore arise, cross this Jordan, you and all this people, to the land which I am giving to them, to the sons of Israel....Be strong and courageous, for you shall give this people possession of the land which I swore to their fathers to give them* (Joshua 1:2,6 NASB).

Because they were ready to obey, they were ready to go in and possess the land. They were determined, This time we will not turn back. This time we will possess what is rightly ours, the land that was promised to us.

Walking through Diane's illness with her and adjusting to life without her after she was gone were seasons of process in my life. But now those difficult seasons have brought me to a new place in my life with God. You have also experienced times when you were in a season of process, but those times have brought you to a season of possession. The process in the desert has brought you to the river that you will cross to possess your promise. You have endured much. You have suffered. You have been hungry. You have been afflicted. But now you are ready to enter into a new season when your tears will be wiped away and you will enter into your destiny. The shadow has disappeared. The clouds have dissipated. Now is the time to receive the promise.

You are not going to negotiate for it. You are not going to beg for it. You are going to take it. It is yours because of a divine promise. As it was for Israel, so it is for you. This is your season and you are not going to miss it this time. You are going to receive all that God has promised to you.

You are still alive, and this is your moment. The cloud has dissipated. The tears have been wiped away. The sorrow has dissolved in the arms of His love. He loves you so much. You are still alive for this moment. He preserved you for this day. The word in the wilderness is now a reality.

ENDNOTE

1. T.S. Eliot, *Collected Poems* (New York: Harcourt Brace and Company, 1962), 81-82.

Epilogue

While life since Diane's death has not always been easy, it has been a continuous process of healing and restoration. Since Diane's passing, my executive assistant's husband, a cancer survivor who Diane affectionately referred to as "Coach," has also died. Nevertheless, I press on in faith knowing that God really does work all things together for the good, and I'm a better man in every area of my life not in spite of what I endured, but because of it.

When I was awakened by the awkward timing of a 4:00 A.M. call that fateful Sunday morning, I knew life would never be the same—and it hasn't been. And as we've traveled, metaphorically, through this "week" together, we've come full circle. Now our journeys begin again, yours and mine. It's early Sunday morning all over again. For me, it's time to make some last-minute adjustments to the sermon I'll deliver five times today, time to prepare for the "week" ahead, and time to reflect on the "week" past. With the "week" I've just had, I think I'll begin this one with a prayer. You should do the same.

"Lord, thank You for allowing me to see another day. I have a deepening appreciation, now more than ever, for the reality that this life is not the end, an appreciation that You are eternal, and You created life to be everlasting. It's only in that truth that I'm able to find comfort in life's tragic mysteries. It's only in that truth that I'm convinced that Diane is gone, but not dead; that I'm alone, but not alone. As I go into this 'week' with the reality that Sundays keep coming, irrespective of what happens between them, please accept my gratitude for allowing me to live the overcoming *life between Sundays,* and allow all those reading this to experience that same overcoming power to walk out the 'week' ahead in victory, not defeat. And now, as I recite some of Diane's favorite verses from Psalm 119, may You use them to bring light and life in places where before there was only darkness and death":

> *I am a stranger on earth; do not hide Your commands from me.*
> *Your statutes are my delight; they are my counselors.*
> *I am laid low in the dust; preserve my life according to Your word.*
> *My soul is weary with sorrow; strengthen me according to Your word.*
> *I have chosen the way of truth; I have set my heart on Your laws.*
> *Fulfill Your promise to Your servant, so that You may be feared.*
> *Remember Your word to Your servant, for You have given me hope.*
> *My comfort in my suffering is this: Your promise preserves my life.*
> *Your word, O Lord, is eternal; it stands firm in the heavens* (Psalm 119:19;24-25;28;30;38;49-50;89)
> *Amen.*

Diane's absolute favorite chapter in Scripture was Psalm 119. I included it above to remind us all that the Living Word of Truth endures forever. Circumstances come and go. We are born and we die. The Word lives on forever. Let this Word water the garden of your soul and prompt you to rise another day.

EPILOGUE

For Diane: Gone, Yet Alive Forever . . .

Additional copies of this book and other
book titles from DESTINY IMAGE are
available at your local bookstore.

Call toll-free: 1-800-722-6774.

Send a request for a catalog to:

Destiny Image® **Publishers, Inc.**
P.O. Box 310
Shippensburg, PA 17257-0310

"Speaking to the Purposes of God for This
Generation and for the Generations to Come."

For a complete list of our titles,
visit us at www.destinyimage.com.